VISIONS

Staff Development Handbook

- Overview of the *Visions* Program
- Organization of *Visions Basic* and *Visions A, B,* and *C*
- Teaching with the *Visions* Program
- Strategies and Techniques

Australia ◇ Canada ◇ Mexico ◇ Singapore ◇ United Kingdom ◇ United States

VISIONS
STAFF DEVELOPMENT HANDBOOK

Publisher: *Phyllis Dobbins*
Director of Development: *Anita Raducanu*
Director, ELL Training and Development: *Evelyn Nelson*
Associate Developmental Editor: *Kasia Zagorski*
Associate Developmental Editor: *Yeny Kim*
Assistant Editor: *Audra Longert*
Production Supervisor: *Mike Burggren*
Marketing Manager: *Jim McDonough*
Manufacturing Manager: *Marcia Locke*
Development: *Weston Editorial*
Design and Production: *Proof Positive/Farrowlyne Associates, Inc.*
Cover Designer: *Studio Montage*
Printer: *Malloy*

Printed in the United States of America.
1 2 3 4 5 6 7 8 9 10 08 07 06 05 04

For more information, contact Heinle, 25 Thomson Place, Boston, Massachusetts 02210 USA, or you can visit our Internet site at http://www.heinle.com

For permission to use material from this text or product contact us:
Tel 1-800-730-2214
Fax 1-800-730-2215
Web www.thomsonrights.com

ISBN: 0-8384-5356-2

Contents

MODULE I Overview of *Visions* Program

 *Visions* Components-at-a-Glance

Visions A, B, and *C* and *Visions Basic Language and Literacy* provide a comprehensive and effective language and language arts program for learners. At each level, *Visions* affords students accessible, authentic readings that are a balance of high-interest fiction and nonfiction, including excerpts from novels, short stories, plays, poems, biographies, speeches, diaries, and content-based informational texts.

Student Components

The core student component for *Visions A, B,* and *C* are full-color hardcover student texts divided into six theme-based units. *Visions Basic,* a full-color hardcover volume as well, contains four introductory chapters that focus on letter-sound relationships and ten theme-based chapters.

Standards-based skills and knowledge taught in the student text are reinforced at each level by both an *Activity Book* and a compendium of helpful learning strategies and reference material in the *Student Handbook.* The *Student CD-ROM* provides listening, speaking, and reading practice, and the *Visions Audio CD* or *Audio Tape* with recordings of all student book readings helps develop listening and speaking skills. For additional skill-building activities online, students can go to the *Visions* companion Web site.

Reflecting the broad themes of *Visions A, B,* and *C,* the *Heinle Reading Library* offers 18 classic stories to encourage independent reading. For beginners, **Mini-Readers**—found in the back of the *Basic Activity Book*—provide lively, contemporary stories designed for practice applying new learning in phonics, vocabulary, and grammar.

More Grammar Practice workbooks reinforce grammar skills identified in the standards. Both the *Basic Newbury House Dictionary* and the *Newbury House Dictionary* are available for *Visions'* users; the latter includes a special pronunciation CD-ROM.

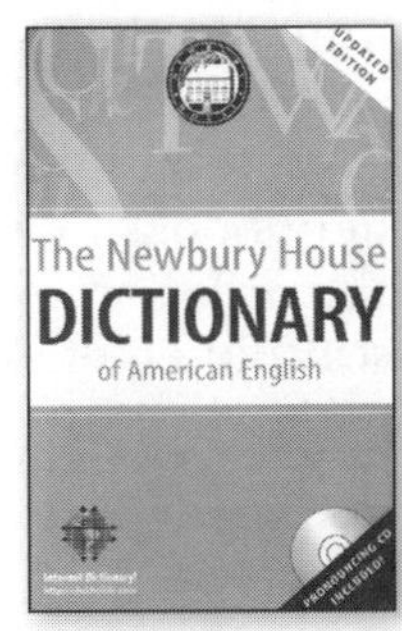

Teacher Components

The *Visions Teacher Editions* are the core component for teachers using *Visions A, B,* or *C.* They contain extensive teaching suggestions on pages wrapped around reduced student pages. In addition, the *Visions Teacher Editions* offer frequent ongoing opportunities for assessments and special information on multi-level options, learning styles, connections beyond the classroom, grammar, spelling, and punctuation. *CNN® Video,* featuring thematic news segments, helps build content comprehension through meaningful viewing activities.

Supporting the *Teacher Editions A, B,* and *C* are the *Teacher Resource Books* with daily lesson plans and pacing guide, a wealth of reproducible masters of graphic organizers, brief summaries of all of the student book readings in English and six other languages, and worksheets for school-home connections, also in six other languages. Various rubrics support teachers' evaluation of student performance. Another feature of the *Teacher Resource Books* is the support for the CNN® video segments. The **Video Scripts** and **Viewing Worksheets** aid teachers and students in taking advantage of the authentic video language experiences related to the themes of the book. The full content of the *Teacher Resource Books* is also available on the *Teacher Resource CD-ROMs* for customization.

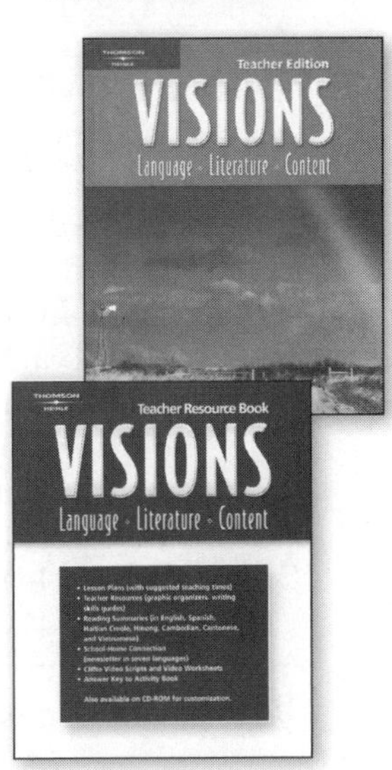

For *Visions Basic,* the *Teacher Resource Book* replaces the *Teacher Edition,* with comprehensive lesson plans, aids for monitoring student progress, teaching suggestions for fluency development, useful reproducible masters of graphic organizers, and instructions for language development activities. **Audioscripts** are incorporated at point of use, as are pointers for pronunciation, language transfer and interference, grammar, spelling, punctuation, and cultural issues.

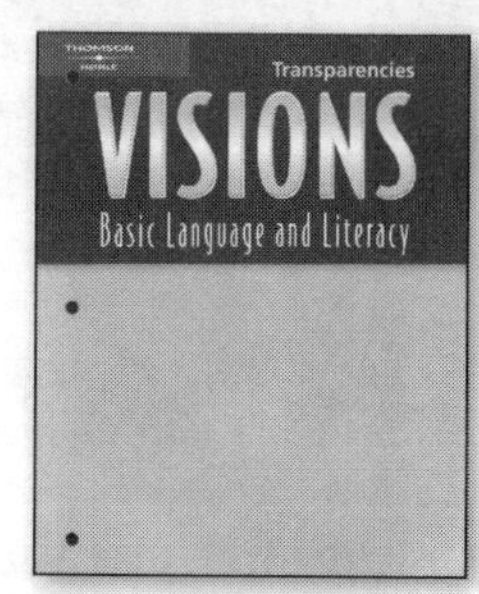

Transparencies of materials in the *Teacher Resource Books* are available to provide alternative presentation methods. For the *Basic* level, supplemental transparencies are provided to support basic student language skill development.

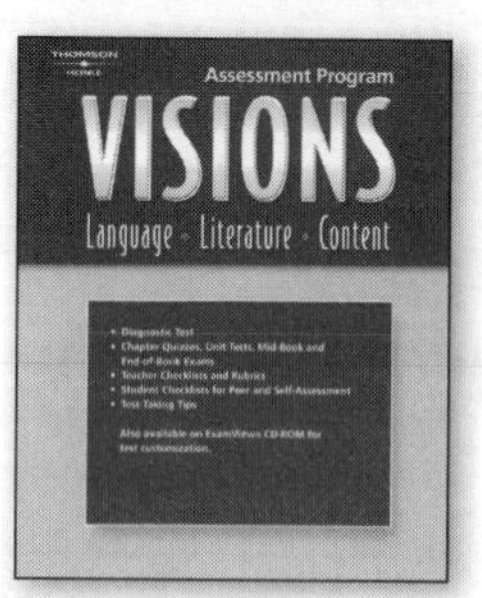

An important teacher component is a complete *Assessment Program* for each level, featuring diagnostic tests and standards-based assessment items that ensure accountability and track student progress. The tests were designed to simulate the standardized tests that many students will be taking. Teachers find the extensive rubrics for student evaluation useful for ongoing assessment and to verify adequate progress. The *Assessment Program* is also available on CD-ROM. Teachers can use *ExamView®* test-generating software to customize their tests by adding, editing, or deleting assessment items.

Other components are this *Staff Development Handbook* and the accompanying *Staff Development Video,* as well as the *Visions* Web site <http://visions.heinle.com> with additional teaching resources and opportunities to share reflections with other teachers online.

Scope and Sequence

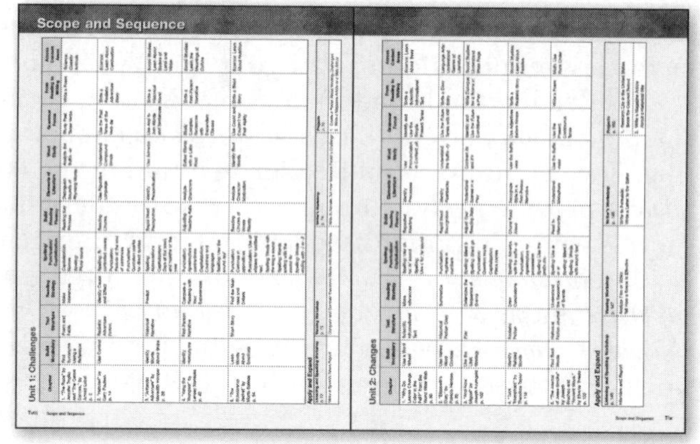

A comprehensive **Scope and Sequence** is found in the front of each *Visions Teacher Edition* and the *Visions Basic Teacher Resource Book.* It outlines all of the elements of the student books. It also allows teachers to discern the order of instruction and the recycling and scaffolding of skills across units.

How Standards Are Covered in *Visions* Components

State standards call for effective language and language arts instruction. *Visions* provides that instruction with opportunities for students to develop competence in the fundamentals of reading and writing; to increase their motivation to achieve in school, at home, and in their communities; and to become lifelong readers and writers.

The *Visions* program was carefully and systematically created to align all instruction with state curricular standards and language arts frameworks. In addition, research-based approaches guide all teaching suggestions, student learning activities and aids, and professional development training. The *Visions* teaching and learning components relate to specific areas of the standards and are reflected in the Modules of this *Staff Development Handbook* as outlined in Table 1.

Table 1. *Visions* Components for Teaching and Learning Skills

For Standards on . . .	Use
Vocabulary Development	Student Book, Teacher Edition, Teacher Resource Book, Activity Book, Student CD-ROM, Student Handbook, Assessment Program, Basic Newbury House Dictionary, Newbury House Dictionary, and Web site
Reading Strategies	Student Book, Teacher Edition, Teacher Resource Book, Activity Book, Transparencies, Student Handbook, Assessment Program, Heinle Reading Library, and Web site
Listening and Speaking	Student Book, Teacher Edition, Teacher Resource Book, Transparencies, Student CD-ROM, Student Handbook, Assessment Program, Newbury House Dictionary and CD-ROM, and Web site
Teaching Reading Fluency	Student Book, Teacher Edition, Teacher Resource Book, Student CD-ROM, Assessment Program, and Newbury House Dictionary and CD-ROM
Teaching Grammar	Student Book, Teacher Edition, Activity Book, Student Handbook, Assessment Program, More Grammar Practice, and Web site
Writing Across Genres	Student Book, Teacher Edition, Teacher Resource Book, Activity Book, Student Handbook, Assessment Program, and Web site
Integrating Technology with Language Learning	Student Book, Teacher Edition, Teacher Resource Book, CNN® Video, Activity Book, Student CD-ROM, Student Handbook, Assessment Program and ExamView® CD-ROM, and Web site
Assessment	Teacher Edition, Activity Book, Student CD-ROM, Student Handbook, and Assessment Program

Within the chapter, the subsections utilize a consistent and logical sequence for ease of use by both teacher and student. In *Visions A, B,* and *C,* there are consistently two sections per page, with a subhead announcing the specific standard or concept being taught in that section. A similar organization with identical terminology is utilized in *Visions Basic,* so that students become familiar with the system as they progress through the program.

Use of Themes in *Visions*

The six units in *Visions A, B,* and *C* are each built around a different broad theme. The purpose of the themes is to provide a conceptual framework for students' language development. Each unit contains four to five chapters that explore the theme through a variety of genres. *Visions Basic* uses a single topic to focus the content of each of the ten chapters. All the themes and topics were chosen for their relevance to and appropriateness for secondary school learners.

Table 2. Themes in the *Visions* Program

Basic		Book A	Book B	Book C
Chapters A. At School B. In the Classroom C. Classmates D. Around the School	Chapters 1. In the School Office 2. About My Family 3. After School 4. Home 5. The Community 6. Food 7. Money 8. Jobs 9. Holidays 10. Feelings	Units 1. Traditions and Culture 2. Environment 3. Conflict and Cooperation 4. Heroes 5. Explorations 6. Connections	Units 1. Challenges 2. Changes 3. Courage 4. Discoveries 5. Communication 6. Frontiers	Units 1. Mysteries 2. Survival 3. Journeys 4. Cycles 5. Freedom 6. Visions

Visions Chapter Schema

In *Visions A, B,* and *C,* each chapter within the theme-based units has a three-part structure: ***Into the Reading,*** the ***Reading Selection,*** and ***Beyond the Reading.*** In *Visions Basic,* each chapter follows a similar but simpler structure while dealing with many of the same standards-based skills.

Note that occasionally a chapter may have two short readings, linked by theme or topic. Appropriate pre- and post-reading activities teach students to account for the similarities and differences between the two readings.

Into the Reading introduces the chapter objectives and helps students relate to the theme through a **Use Prior Knowledge** activity. The **Build Background** section provides a context for the reading with a brief explanation and a map or illustration. The **Content Connection** relates the reading to an academic subject, while **Build Vocabulary** teaches a strategy for approaching essential new words that will be encountered in the reading. On the following page, the reading selection's **Text Structure,** clarified by a graphic organizer, is described, and instructions for learning and applying a **Reading Strategy** to the reading selection follow.

In the *Teacher Editions,* alternative teaching ideas for mixed-ability classes are offered in **Multi-Level Options.** A **Connection** to home, culture, community, or academic subject is explored; and teaching suggestions for different **Learning Styles** are provided. These propose alternative ways to approach the student page materials based on Howard Gardner's theory of multiple intelligences. (2000) **Connection** and **Learning Styles** also appear in ***Beyond the Reading.***

The ***Reading Selection*** is the instructional core of each chapter. It consists of a title page, one or more reading selections, and information about the authors. The readings can be listened to on audiotapes or CD. The *Teacher Resource Books* and *Transparencies* also contain brief summaries of the readings in English and in six other languages. The last page of each reading selection has the author's picture (when available), has a short biographical sketch, and includes higher-order thinking questions for students to answer.

Table 3. *Visions A, B,* and *C*: Chapter Schema

Into the Reading →	Reading Selection →	Beyond the Reading
Objectives Use Prior Knowledge Build Background Content Connection Build Vocabulary Text Structure Reading Strategy	Title Page Reading Selection About the Author	Reading Comprehension (QAR) Build Reading Fluency Listen, Speak, Interact Elements of Literature Word Study Grammar Focus From Reading to Writing Across Content Areas

On these pages, **Multi-Level Options** provides teaching suggestions and level-appropriate comprehension questions about the reading. There is also a spelling, capitalization, or punctuation activity, and on the last page of the reading selection, an opportunity for a self-evaluation called **Evaluate Your Reading Strategy.** Also on the last page, teachers can find an activity called **Across Selections,** which asks students to compare and contrast features of two or more readings.

Beyond the Reading examines students' reading comprehension with factual, inferential, and personal application questions in a **Question-Answer Relationships (QAR)** format, followed by a fluency exercise. On the facing page, listening and speaking skills, which mirror academic oral language tasks, are practiced in **Listen, Speak, Interact.** This is followed by **Elements of Literature**—a section that addresses a specialized literary concept or standard. On the next page, the **Word Study** section helps students analyze vocabulary in detail in accordance with state standards and to prepare for the types of items found on standardized tests. **Grammar Focus** addresses a significant grammar point from the reading, and **From Reading to Writing** brings together major aspects of the chapter's instruction—text structure, genre, vocabulary, and grammar—in a unified, productive writing exercise. Finally, the material in the chapter is broadened to include vocabulary and content connections to other academic subjects in **Across Content Areas.**

Apply and Expand

An ***Apply and Expand*** section can be found at the end of each Unit. It contains **Listening and Speaking, Viewing,** and **Writer's Workshops,** two expansion **Projects,** and suggestions for **Further Reading.** The primary purpose of ***Apply and Expand*** is to give students an opportunity to engage in and apply all aspects of language skills to oral and written presentations related to the theme and content of the unit. It also gives students a chance to evaluate themselves according to standards-based criteria and to set new goals based on their progress.

Students using *Visions Basic* complete each chapter with a writing activity, a skills **Review** and **Assess,** and **Projects** to apply what they have learned.

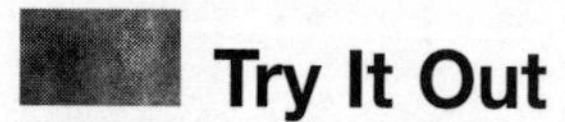

Try It Out

Teacher Activity: Scavenger Hunt

Use the information you learned in Module I, your knowledge of the *Visions* program, and Teacher Edition B to respond to the following items. Write your answers on a separate sheet of paper.

You have 6 minutes to complete as many as you can.

Share your responses in small groups.

Item	Response/Notes
1. How many units are there in each *Visions Student Book* (*A*, *B*, and *C*)?	
2. What information can you find on the first page of any Unit Opener?	
3. What is the three-part structure of each chapter in *Visions Student Book A, B,* and *C?*	
4. What resources can you find on the *Visions Transparencies?*	
5. What skill is addressed in the *first* **Multi-Level Options** in every chapter of *Visions Teacher Edition* (*A, B,* and *C*)?	
6. What five genres are explored in *Visions Student Book B,* Unit 4?	
7. What three **Learning Styles** are addressed in "The Lewis and Clark Expedition" in *Visions Teacher Edition Book B?*	
8. What checklists can your students use? (Record where you find them.)	

Teacher Reflections

With your group, discuss these questions about the Teacher Activity.

1. What were the easiest items to find?
2. Was any part especially difficult? In what way?
3. What did you learn about the *Visions* program during the Scavenger Hunt?
4. How can you adapt this Scavenger Hunt to help your students become familiar with *Visions?*
5. What additional information about *Visions* did you learn from your small group?
6. How do you plan to integrate the various components of *Visions* into your classroom?

MODULE II Organization of *Visions A, B,* and C

Each book in *Visions A, B,* and *C* contains six units. Each unit is comprised of:

1. a two-page unit opener;
2. four or five chapters—the instructional core of the unit; Units 1–3 each have five chapters, and Units 4–6 have four chapters each; and
3. follow-up workshops, projects, and suggested readings entitled ***Apply and Expand.***

A. Introduce the Unit

The two-page unit openers in *Visions A, B,* and *C* present a multifaceted introduction to the unit theme and the chapters that follow. The purpose of the unit openers is to begin to build background information and prepare students for the reading selections that follow.

1. Student Book

On the first unit opener page, students see the unit's title and table of contents. The title is always one or two key words that name a broad thematic concept. The table of contents lists the chapter titles and authors, selection genres, and page numbers.

On the facing page, students view a painting, a photograph, a sculpture, or an artifact that represents an aspect of the unit theme. **View the Picture** contains guided questions about the art. In examining the art, students visually explore the theme as they gain or activate background knowledge and context to prepare for the readings. For visual learners and students with limited language proficiency, the art aids comprehension of abstract themes. Pieces were selected to support the affective domains of learning and to engage students.

2. Teacher Edition

In the *Teacher Edition,* the first page of a unit provides a summary of the unit materials, activities to help students clarify the meaning of the theme, a strategy for examining the table of contents, and the **Unit Objectives.** The list of reading selections in the table of contents provides an opportunity to question students on a variety of levels. These questions can begin with narrow, convergent yes/no questions for newcomers, and move with increasing complexity to divergent, open-ended questions for advanced students. Use the table of contents to explain what an excerpt is and to ask about genres that students may have already encountered, such as poems and informational texts. Teachers can use the table of contents in subsequent units to tie in and tie back to these earlier readings.

On the second page, **View the Picture** provides background information about the artist or the artwork. The type of art medium used, the historical context, the style and subject are among the kinds of information that can help students interpret the art, think about the theme, and prepare for reading. A variety of activities encourage students to describe and interpret what they see, speculate about form, line, and color, and discuss whether the art is realistic or not. Cross-curricular links to elective or required art courses can be made. Students can be encouraged to create their own art or respond to the image portrayed.

In **Connect to the Theme,** students are asked to discuss their own experiences with, or knowledge of, the unit theme. This is the students' first opportunity to connect the readings to their own experience, which Cummins (1994) pointed out is a critical step in the pre-reading process.

This section concludes with an **Assess** in which students are asked to respond briefly to the unit theme and the material covered on those two pages. They may be asked to draw a picture, create an artifact, or describe or write about an aspect of the unit theme.

3. Unit Objectives

Across the bottom pages of the opener, the *Teacher Edition* lists key objectives from five skill areas in each chapter of the unit—Reading, Listening and Speaking, Grammar, Writing, and Content—for easy reference. These are also tracked in the Skills Index in the back of the *Teacher Edition.* The objectives assist in both ensuring that students meet required standards and tracking their completion. Throughout the *Visions* program, these objectives will be recycled and expanded in more and more complex ways.

B. Into the Reading

Visions is based on the view that pre-teaching and post-reading activities increase reading comprehension and appreciation of the text, and can enhance the acquisition of language that students will need to succeed academically. Hence, *Visions* has a three-part structure: ***Into the Reading,*** the ***Reading Selection,*** and ***Beyond the Reading.***

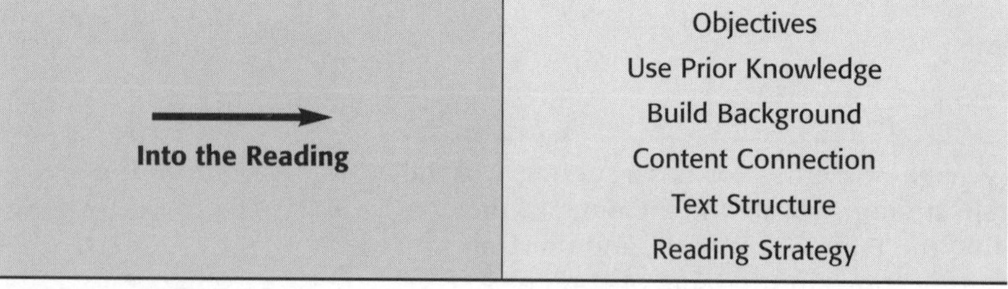

1. Chapter Objectives

Each chapter begins with a list of key skill-area objectives. They reflect the subheads in each section and are written in student-friendly language. Research shows that learners who have a sense of the instructional goals tend to be more successful. In the *Teacher Editions,* a brief suggestion is offered for examining the objectives with the students so that they will know what they can expect to accomplish. These objectives signal the chapter's reading strategy and selection; a listening and speaking skill; the grammar concept being taught; and a related science, math, language arts, social studies, or fine arts topic. The chapter subheads (e.g., **Share Knowledge** or **Use Context**) reflect state teaching and learning standards. This section can be revisited at the end of the chapter so that students can confirm their learning.

2. Use Prior Knowledge

Students are drawn into the chapter with a **Use Prior Knowledge** activity. The purposes of this section are to:

a. draw on students' prior knowledge to help them understand new information in the chapter reading;

b. relate content to personal experiences and feelings;

c. provide students with organizing techniques for visually representing their ideas and experiences, including word webs, sunshine organizers, lists, and charts;

d. encourage students to record and share their knowledge with partners;

e. expose students to cultural differences; and

f. begin preparing students to achieve the final writing activity in the chapter.

In some cases, students may have no prior experience with the topic, so care is given to work from the known to the unknown, drawing on related knowledge.

3. Build Background

Each reading in the *Visions* program is preceded by an activity to help students gain background information specific to the reading selection. **Build Background** sets a context for comprehension of the reading through a brief explanation, map, chart, or illustration. The **Content Connection** box provides a key fact about a related academic area. Each *Teacher Edition* contains questions and information to guide discussion and exploration of the background information.

4. Build Vocabulary

Learning vocabulary is more than memorizing words or their meanings. It is the recognition and production of meaningful language within a specific context (Lindsay, 2000). To accomplish this, English language learners need to learn at least 2,000 high-frequency words, or about 80 percent of the words we regularly read or hear (Decarrico, 2001). Students also need the tools to acquire specialized content-area vocabularies. As part of *Visions*' instruction in vocabulary development, **Build Vocabulary:**

a. introduces the topical vocabulary such as science terms, vivid verbs, and contextualized words that scaffold the chapter reading;

b. draws on the students' personal experiences to bring meanings to words in context such as interpreting idioms, multiple-meaning words, and understanding words from context;

c. provides students with organizing techniques and strategies for learning or remembering new vocabulary, including word squares, the LINK strategy, and note-taking;

d. teaches students to use multiple reference aids, including standard and online reference books, thesauruses, and the CD-ROM dictionary to examine homonyms, locate definitions, distinguish denotative and connotative meaning, and clarify pronunciation; and

e. encourages students to maintain a Personal Dictionary for their new vocabulary.

In the *Visions Teacher Editions,* the teacher is always provided with **Multi-Level Options** for the **Build Vocabulary** section on the facing page. **Multi-Level Options** offer a variety of strategies for teaching and using **Build Vocabulary** with heterogeneously grouped classes of newcomer, beginning, intermediate, and advanced students. Additional practice of the skills and content introduced in **Build Vocabulary** is offered on the *Student CD-ROM* and in the *Activity Book.*

5. Connections and Learning Styles

In the *Visions Teacher Editions,* on both ***Into the Reading*** and ***Beyond the Reading*** pages, teachers can find **Content, Home, Cultural,** or **Community Connection** activities. These are based either on academic subjects, including the **Arts** and **Technology,** or on more personal links to students' home, community, and culture. The academic **Connections** bring a specialized, content-laden perspective to the reading. The **Home, Community,** and **Cultural Connection** activities provide opportunities for family involvement, suggest activities or speakers, or present ways to share diverse experiences. These latter **Connections** also promote tolerance and understanding and draw on the richness of diversity as they demonstrate links between the reading and students' lives.

Learning Styles proposes alternative teaching approaches based on the theory posited by Howard Gardner (2000) that people learn in different ways through multiple intelligences—verbal, mathematical, visual, musical, kinesthetic, interpersonal, intrapersonal, and natural.

6. Text Structure: Genre Schema

Text Structure introduces and analyzes the distinguishing features of the reading selection's genre. Literary terms are examined following state standards, and in preparation for standardized achievement testing. These features are practiced later in each chapter in ***Beyond the Reading's*** **From Reading to Writing** section. These concepts are important for student success in the mainstream academic curriculum. A list of these text structures can be found in each *Teacher Edition* in the **Scope and Sequence,** pages Tviii–Txiii. The *Student CD-ROM* contains additional reinforcement of each chapter's target text structure.

7. Reading Strategy

Into the Reading in *Visions A, B,* and *C* concludes by focusing on strategies to help students improve their reading comprehension. Key elements of strategies are defined, explained, and modeled. Students then practice the strategy before beginning the reading selection. The strategy is highlighted throughout the reading by guide questions in the text margins. These questions allow students to practice their use of the strategy. This application practice encourages internalization of the strategy, so that it can be successfully applied to new reading material.

On the bottom of the *Teacher Edition* pages, the **Multi-Level Options** offers alternative teaching suggestions for either the **Text Structure** or **Reading Strategy** sections at four proficiency levels, from newcomer to advanced. Additional practice of the skills introduced in this section can be found on the *Student CD-ROM.*

C. The Reading Selection

Throughout *Visions,* active reading strategies are taught, practiced, and refined to provide students with the skills needed to meet grade-level standards. *Visions* offers accessible, authentic literature, including fiction and nonfiction, with multilevel activity options to meet the needs of all students. The ***Reading Selection,*** the core of each *Visions* chapter, consists of a title page, one or more reading selections, and information about the authors.

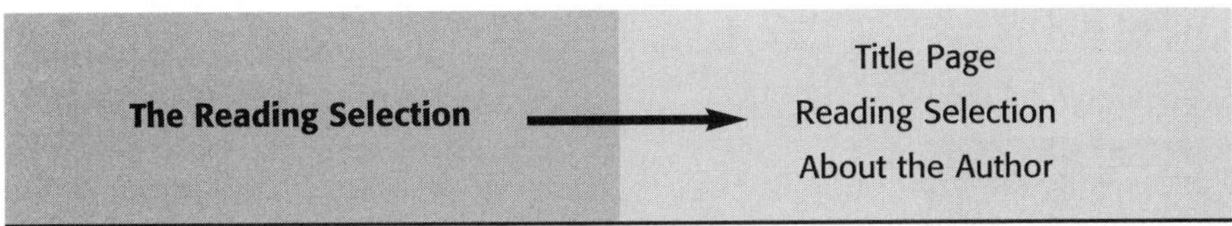

1. Reading Selection Title Page

In the *Student Book,* the reading selection title page includes the selection title(s), author(s), genre identification, and a related graphic designed to aid anticipation and comprehension.

The *Teacher Editions* contain a list of **Reading Selection Materials** that can be used at this point, plus ways to **Preview the Selection.** The two most important components of the materials list are the audiotapes or CDs and the reading summaries in the *Teacher Resource Books* and on *Transparencies.* The reading summary can be read prior to the selection to help students understand what they are about to read in detail. Another application of the reading summary is to create a cloze exercise and have students guess missing vocabulary. Other options are listed in the teacher notes. In **Preview the Selection,** teaching suggestions offer an opportunity to discuss the title, art, genre, and author, and their potential relation to the unit theme, which in turn reinforces similar activities previously used with the art in the unit introduction.

2. Reading Selection

Each chapter contains one or two ***Reading Selections*** from a wide variety of genres. These selections are chosen to develop comprehension, vocabulary, a reading strategy, and fluency. In each reading, text features designed to support these skills include: numbered paragraphs or stanzas, captioned graphics, key vocabulary glosses, and guide questions focusing on applications of the reading strategy. The guide question "pointers" direct students to places in the reading where they may practice the reading strategy.

3. About the Author

The last page of each ***Reading Selection*** has the author's picture and a short biographical sketch called **About the Author.** Students are asked to respond to this information, using higher-order thinking to analyze issues, such as the author's purpose, challenge, and feelings, and to synthesize their own reaction to the reading.

In the *Teacher Editions,* **Multi-Level Options** provides teaching suggestions and level-appropriate comprehension questions on the reading. There are also contextualized spelling, capitalization, or punctuation activities drawn from the reading. These are practiced further in the *Activity Book* and/or on the *Student CD-ROM.*

On the last page of the ***Reading Selection,*** there is an opportunity for a self-evaluation called **Evaluate Your Reading Strategy.** This self-assessment activity allows students to think critically about their own skills and progress and reflect on how well they applied the reading strategy to increase their comprehension of the reading text.

Teachers can also find an activity on this page called **Across Selections,** which asks students to compare features or aspects of this reading with one or more earlier readings.

D. Beyond the Reading

Beyond the Reading →	Reading Comprehension (QAR) Build Reading Fluency Listen, Speak, Interact Elements of Literature Word Study Grammar Focus From Reading to Writing Across Content Areas

1. Reading Comprehension (QAR)

The first section of ***Beyond the Reading*** in *Visions A, B,* and *C* is **Reading Comprehension,** which uses the **Question-Answer Relationship** (QAR) strategy for evaluating students' understanding of the ***Reading Selection.***

According to the California Department of Education, the QAR strategy helps students classify questions and locate answers to them. Moreover, it recognizes that reading is a dynamic process involving the reader, the text, and the context. To apply the QAR strategy, students learn to recognize the relationship between a specific type of question and where they can go in the text to find an answer to it. This is a critical skill for enhancing comprehension in content areas.

The **Question-Answer Relationship** section begins with **"Right There"**—literal questions that check factual recall. Next, students respond to inferential questions in **"Think and Search."** Here students formulate answers by searching relevant passages and integrating information from different parts of the text. Finally, evaluative questions in

Higher Order Thinking Skills
Question-Answer Relationships (QAR)

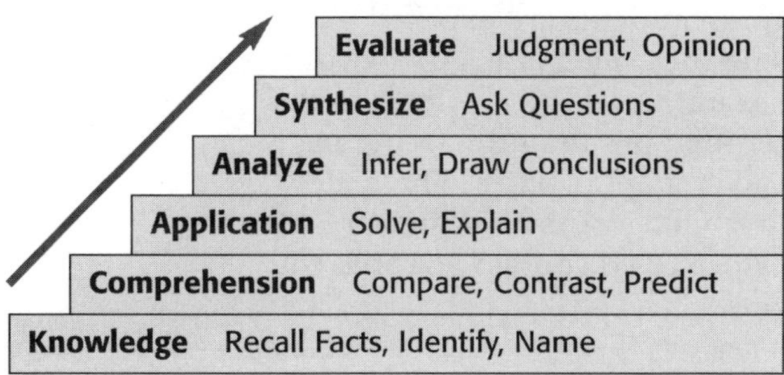

Bloom's Taxonomy

"Author and You" and **"On Your Own"** help students develop higher order thinking skills (Fowler, 2003). In **"Author and You,"** students answer questions by combining information that they already know with author statements in the text. In **"On Your Own,"** students use personal knowledge and experience to state an opinion or elaborate on information. These **Question-Answer Relationships** are illustrated in the Bloom's Taxonomy graphic.

2. Reading Fluency

The National Reading Panel (2002) defines fluency as "the ability to read a text quickly, accurately, and with proper expression" and implicit comprehension. Research has further shown that directed oral reading practice with repetition works even more effectively than silent reading because students benefit from the involvement and feedback of peers, teachers, tutors, and parents. To encourage and enhance reading, *Visions* contains an explicit fluency-building exercise in **Build Reading Fluency** as part of ***Beyond the Reading.*** Each chapter offers an exercise such as chunking, rapid word recognition, echo reading, reading with audio, oral reading, adjusting reading rate, assisted reading, paired reading, reading for speed, reading for expression, and repeated reading.

3. Listen, Speak, Interact

This component of each chapter appears on the second page of ***Beyond the Reading*** in *Visions A, B,* and *C.* It guides students to discuss and interact with others by sharing ideas, personal experiences, and reactions to the reading selection. It is authentic listening and speaking and students often take notes on ideas and information shared by their partners.

Listen, Speak, Interact gives students an opportunity to take risks as they express themselves for authentic purposes (Hedge, 2001), including giving opinions, describing things, giving instructions, describing a process, giving explanations, and supporting arguments (Gibbons, 1993).

In cooperative groupings, students practice and refine their listening and speaking skills by performing dialogues, presenting dramatic readings, acting out poems, role-playing interviews, practicing intonation, and discussing values. These guided listening and speaking tasks prepare students for the types of academic listening and speaking assignments they face in mainstream classes.

4. Elements of Literature

The second page of ***Beyond the Reading*** in *Visions A, B,* and *C* highlights and explains discrete elements of literature. Students are exposed to essential terms and language for discussing these elements. An activity guides students to recognize or identify examples of the elements in the reading selection. **Multi-Level Options** on the bottom of the facing page of the *Teacher Edition* offers additional teaching approaches. These elements reflect those found in mainstream language arts and English courses. Both the *Activity Book* and *Student CD-ROM* contain activities for each chapter that reinforce these elements.

5. Word Study

For efficient methods of acquiring clusters of new words instead of individual words, Schmitt (1997) recommends learning word families and building word associations from roots and affixes. For example, learning the root *act* will help students understand and learn words derived from it, such as *action, active, activate,* and *actor.* To assist in learning these methods and following state standards, and to expose students to skills that are regularly taught, applied, and tested in mainstream curriculum, *Visions* includes **Word Study** to help students:

a. understand multiple-meaning words;

b. recognize and use roots and affixes;

c. distinguish denotative and connotative meanings;

d. recognize word origins and historical influences on English words;

e. identify Greek and Latin roots;

f. recognize and use figurative language and modifiers;

g. use multiple reference aids (thesaurus, synonym finder, dictionary, software); and

h. recognize and use contractions.

The *Student CD-ROM* and the *Activity Book* each contain additional reinforcement of these skills for each chapter.

6. Grammar Focus

Research strongly suggests that pre-adolescent and adolescent learners need to focus on grammar to help them develop accuracy in their academic use of the language. Students at this age understand and often welcome analytic descriptions of grammatical patterns and rules in their writing. They also appreciate having their errors noted at appropriate moments and being taught useful substitutions and explanations.

In general, research supports the following principles of teaching grammar in context.

a. Expose students to high-quality literature that provides syntactic challenges.

b. Have students write as frequently as possible and provide them with feedback on both content and use of language.

c. Select and teach elements of grammar that students encounter in their content reading and need in the revision stage of their writing.

d. Use their writing as diagnostic tools to determine aspects of grammar they need to learn or are ready to learn, and make these part of instruction.

e. Base this instruction on a process that moves from demonstration through structured practice to free practice, coupled with meaningful feedback.
f. Teach students to use grammatical conventions and terminology in order to provide a common "language" of grammar.
g. Emphasize aspects of grammar that help students to communicate more effectively and use conventional mechanics and appropriate language.

(Adapted from Celce-Murcia, 1991)

Grammar Focus encompasses a wide range of language arts standards that include parts of speech, tenses, clauses and sentences, negatives and contractions, word order, comparative and superlative adjectives, pronoun referents, modals, and related punctuation and spelling rules.

Two pages of grammar review and reinforcement can be found in the *Visions Activity Book* for all levels. In these books, a verbal and a graphic explanation of the grammar point are presented, followed by structured, and then less structured, activities. For independent review and reference, the *Visions Student Handbook* contains handy summaries of all grammar and usage points. Additionally, *More Grammar Practice* is available for each level, and grammar practice is supported on the *Student CD-ROM* and in the *Activity Book.*

Mindful that accurate grammar is a component, not a goal, of the acquisition of academic content and effective communication, *Visions* integrates the grammar instruction of **Grammar Focus** with applications in **From Reading to Writing** that follows.

7. From Reading to Writing

From Reading to Writing is a critical section of each chapter. In this section, students apply all parts of the chapter's instruction. They employ all aspects of the material they studied throughout the chapter—prior knowledge, using models of text structure, new vocabulary, using significant grammar, revising and editing, and above all, utilizing content—to create a unified, productive writing exercise.

Every chapter provides this practice, so that students have ample opportunities to improve their all-important writing skills. The *Activity Book* also provides opportunities for practice.

8. Across Content Areas

Visions A, B, and *C* conclude each chapter with **Across Content Areas,** an exercise that moves beyond the chapter content to an examination of a related topic in math, science, language arts, the arts, or social studies. The primary purposes of **Across Content Areas** are to expand and extend vocabulary concepts into wider academic areas and to recycle vocabulary and concepts from previous chapters or units. It exposes students to additional models of content-area reading types and allows them to gain confidence in dealing with expository reading above and beyond the chapter readings. This concluding section also addresses the fundamental standard that students be able to attack and understand new vocabulary and concepts across content areas. The *Activity Book* contains additional content-area exploration activities.

Try It Out

Teacher Activity: Using Higher Order Thinking Skills

Participants each need a blank **Two-Column Chart,** found in the *Teacher Resource Book,* page 44, or on *Transparency* #10. They may also refer to "Bloom's Taxonomy" on page 13. Write the higher order thinking skills down the left column of the chart. In the right column, for each skill, write one question about Module II that requires use of that skill to answer.

Teacher Reflections

Share the questions in small groups and discuss your answers.

1. Which types of questions were easier to develop? Were they also easier to answer? Would students find them easier, too?
2. Which types of questions were harder to create and answer? Why?
3. How can you use this activity with your students?
4. How does this activity relate to the standards you must meet?

MODULE III Teaching with *Visions A, B,* and C

This module presents a practical, step-by-step guide for implementing *Visions A, B,* or *C* in the classroom. The sample chapter below used to model teaching is Chapter 3, "Antarctic Adventure" from *Visions Book B,* Unit 1: *Challenges.* This module will do the following:

1. explain procedures and provide suggestions for teaching *Visions A, B,* and *C;*
2. show how the Unit Opener introduces the broad unit theme and how the chapter readings relate to that theme;
3. provide a "walk-through" of a typical chapter, so that teachers new to *Visions* can learn how to teach it and to use each component effectively; and
4. provide a "walk-through" of the end-of-unit ***Apply and Expand*** activities.

A. Introduce the Unit

(*Book B, Teacher Edition*, pages xii–1)

➤ Go to: *Book B, Teacher Edition,* Unit 1, pages xii–1

This two-page unit opener launches the broad unit theme, *Challenges.* Each unit opener helps build background information and prepare students for the reading selections that follow.

1. Unit Materials (*Book B, Teacher Edition*, page xii)

Be sure to gather the books and material of the *Visions* program listed here. Bookmark the relevant pages.

For teaching strategies, watch the *Staff Development Video* that accompanies *Visions.*

You can supplement this part of the unit with examples of art from other books or from the Internet. For the theme of *Challenges,* find additional pictures of people facing challenges such as mountain climbers, the Wright brothers working on their flying machine, doctors operating on patients, etc. Remember that not all challenges are physical: in fact, most of the challenges your students face are social or emotional, so pictures of teens taking a test or parking a car may also be appropriate.

2. Unit Theme: *Challenges* (*Book B, Teacher Edition*, page xii)

See suggestions in the side column of the *Teacher Edition,* page xii. Write *Challenges* on the board. Say the word or have an advanced student read it aloud. Have students find and point to the word in their books.

Option A To clarify the meaning of *Challenges,* bring in several pictures of people dealing with difficult challenges such as biking up a steep mountain, running a marathon, steering a boat in a storm, a person in a wheelchair looking up a flight of stairs, etc.

Hold up the pictures one at a time.

> ***Say:*** *This is a* challenge.
>
> Then hold up one or two pictures of people doing something easy like eating ice cream or watching a parade. ***Say:*** *This is* not *a challenge. Is a challenge easy or hard?* (hard) Mix up challenging and easy pictures and hold them up one at a time. For each picture, ***ask:*** *Is this a challenge?*

Select one challenging picture to use as a model, for example, biking up a mountain.

> ***Say:*** *This is a challenge because it's hard to ride a bicycle uphill. You get hot and tired. You have to be strong. You have to work hard. This is* not *easy!*
>
> *Think about your first day at school. What challenges do new students face? What challenges do you face in school or in your neighborhood?* (making friends, learning English, finding the right bus stop)

Respond to student answers with comments like, *That's right. Interesting example. Can you tell me more? Does anyone else have a challenge like that?*

Your goal is comprehension. You can "correct" indirectly by modeling the correct forms of vocabulary or pronunciation, without requiring that students produce the accurate forms.

Option B Do a Think-Pair-Share to stimulate thinking about the theme of *Challenges* and to tie the theme back to students' experiences.

> ***Say:*** *Think about a challenge you faced. Or one that someone you know faced. For example, moving to a new home is a big challenge. What was the challenge you faced? What made it a challenge? How did you feel about it?*
>
> *After you think about the challenge, work in pairs. Take turns telling about your challenge. Listen carefully as your partner talks. Write notes to help you remember.*
>
> *Finally, talk with another pair. Each person takes a turn retelling his or her* partner's *story. Then pick one story from your small group to share with the class.*

3. Unit Preview: Table of Contents (*Book B, Teacher Edition*, page xii)

Option A Use the Unit 1 table of contents on this page (page xii) to introduce your students to the reading selections in the unit. Make an overhead transparency of this page, so that students can follow along.

> ***Say:*** *The readings in this unit are about different kinds of challenges. Where do you find the* readings *in this unit?* (in the table of contents)
>
> To check for understanding, ***say:*** *Point to the table of contents on this page. What do you find in the table of contents?* (chapter numbers, page numbers, titles, authors, poem, fable, narrative, etc.)

Read the first two reading selection titles aloud. Point to words as you say them. ***Say:*** *Chapter 1 has two reading selections.* The Race *is a poem by Jennifer Trujillo.* The Camel Dances *is a fable by Arnold Lobel.*

Have volunteers continue reading the rest of the table of contents aloud. If you use a transparency, beginning or intermediate students can point to the words as they are read.

Option B Explore the table of contents on page xii with your students by asking questions of various levels from narrow, convergent yes/no questions through higher-level divergent questions.

Ask: *Is* The Race *in Chapter 2?* (no) *Is* The Camel Dances *a poem or a fable?* (fable) *Who wrote* Antarctic Adventure? (Meredith Hooper) *What chapter starts on page 54?* (Chapter 5) *What kinds of readings are in the* Challenges *unit?* (poem, fable, excerpts of novel, historical narrative, short story) *What makes something challenging?* (sample answer: Not many people can do it.)

Option C Teach key vocabulary. Bring in a copy of the novel, *Hatchet.*

Write: *excerpts* ***Say:*** *Three readings are* excerpts. *Can you name the readings?* (*Hatchet, Antarctic Adventure, Yang the Youngest*) *Does anyone know what an excerpt is?* If not, explain it by handing the novel to a student. ***Ask:*** *How many pages is* Hatchet? ***Write:*** Hatchet: (number) *pages.* ***Say:*** *Now, class, turn to page 17. This is the excerpt of* Hatchet. *How many pages is the excerpt?* (7) ***Write:*** *excerpt of* Hatchet: *7 pages.* ***Ask:*** *Is an excerpt a whole book?* (no) *Is an excerpt a part of a book?* (yes)

Now turn to the Table of Contents again.

Ask: *Are we reading all of* Antarctic Adventure *and* Yang the Youngest? (no) *What are we reading from* Antarctic Adventure? (an excerpt) *How much of* Yang the Youngest *is in our books?* (sample answer: an excerpt)

4. View the Picture (*Book B, Teacher Edition,* page 1)

See additional suggestions and notes in the side column of the *Teacher Edition,* page xii.

Option A Before discussing the heading and questions under the artwork, ask students about the picture.

Ask: *Do you see boys in the picture?* (yes) *What are they doing?* (running) *What is the title of the picture?* (Runners) *Who is the artist?* (Robert Delaunay) *Is this a painting or a photograph?* (painting)

Direct students to the heading, **View the Picture**, on page 1. Read it aloud.

Ask: *What does* view *mean?*

If students aren't sure, explain what *view* means with the following exercise.

Word	**Symbol**
View	
Meaning	**Sentence**

Draw a Word Square on the board or on poster paper with *view* in the Word box. Give students blank copies of the Word Square graphic organizer from the *Teacher Resource Book*, page 41. Have them copy *view* and put the Word Squares aside.

First, mime looking carefully at the picture. Emphasize that you are looking at it by making a line in the air from your eyes to the page. Then do this Think Aloud.

> ***Say:*** View *the picture. Hmmm. I know what* view *means. I am* viewing *the picture right now. Now class, can you* view (something on a bulletin board)? *What else do you want to* view? Have volunteers direct the class to "view" different parts of, or items in, the room. Monitor that everyone is getting that to *view* means to *look at.* ***Ask:*** *What words mean the same as* view?

Write one or two synonyms that students suggest in the Meaning box (sample synonyms: *see, look*). Then draw a pair of eyes in the Symbol box.

> ***Say:*** *A picture of eyes helps me remember what* view *means. What things help you remember the meaning of* view? (a magnifying glass, binoculars, etc.) *Draw them in your Word Square.*

Direct students to complete their Word Squares by copying the direction *View the Picture* from the book or creating their own sentence in the Sentence box. Have volunteers show their symbols and read their sentences aloud.

Option B Direct students to the questions under **View the Picture.**

> ***Say:*** *I'm going to read the questions. Think about them and tell a partner your answers.* Allow your students to talk for two or three minutes as you circulate and monitor their conversations.

Then read the paragraph below the questions.

Option C Read or summarize the information about Delaunay provided in the *Teacher Edition* under **1. Art background.** If you talk about the Impressionists or Cubists, bring in examples of works by Monet, Renoir, Picasso, or Braque. Or do an Internet search with your students for other examples.

Option D Follow the suggestions in the *Teacher Edition* for **2. Art interpretation.** Teach vocabulary words or simplify the questions for newcomers or beginning students.

(a) Explore style

To teach the word *blurry*, draw a clear, straight line with chalk or a pencil. Write *clear* under it. Then draw a fuzzy line with the side of the chalk or pencil. Write *blurry* under it. Say the words as you point to each line.

> ***Ask:*** *Is the painting clear or blurry?* (blurry) *What colors do you see?* (sample answers: blue, red, etc.) *Why did the painter make the runners blurry?* (sample answer: to show how fast they're running)

(b) Interpret the painting

Ask: *Are the runners running on a track or on grass?* (track) *How do the runners feel?* (sample answers: hopeful, hot) *Who do you think will win?* (sample answer: the boy in blue) *Why do you think that?* (sample answer: He's running fast.)

(c) Connect to the theme

Say: *The unit theme is challenges. Talk to the person next to you. Talk about the challenges you see in the painting.* Give students 2–3 minutes to talk. Then, ***ask:*** *What challenges did you talk about?*

6. 

(*Book B, Teacher Edition*, page 1)

Have students do the activity in the **Assess** on page 1. Help them write labels or captions. Post the drawings on a class bulletin board. In small groups, volunteers can present their drawings and explain their artwork. Use the **Rubric for Oral Presentations** found in the *Assessment Program,* page 137.

B. Into the Reading

(*Book B, Teacher Edition*, pages 28–30)

➤ Go to: *Book B, Teacher Edition,* Unit 1, Chapter 3, page 28

This walk-through provides sample instructions for the pre-reading instruction and activities of a typical chapter in *Visions A, B,* and *C.*

1. Chapter Materials (*Book B, Teacher Edition*, page 28)

Be sure to gather the books and materials needed for the chapter. For example, bookmark pages 17–24 in the *Activity Book.*

2. Objectives (*Book B, Teacher Edition*, page 28)

See suggestions for teaching **Objectives** in the side column of the *Teacher Edition,* page 28.

Option A Do a partner read aloud of the **Objectives.** Model the activity with a student. Sit facing each other with your books opened. Tell the student to read aloud the first skill area. Point to it and **prompt:** *Reading,* if needed. Then read the objective. Pretend to have difficulty with a word and ask your partner for help.

Say: *Predict events as you read a. . . . Uh, what's that word?* Let the student read it for you. Then repeat the complete objective. ***Say:*** *Predict events as you read a historical narrative.*

Then read the next skill area to the student. ***Say:*** *Listening and Speaking*

Look up and indicate to the student to read the objective. Assist as needed.

Option B Objectives can be examined in various ways from chapter to chapter by doing a teacher read aloud, reading chorally, assigning five groups to present one objective each to the class, etc. Spend a few minutes on **Objectives.** At the end of the chapter, go back and review these objectives with the class to show students what they have accomplished.

3. Use Prior Knowledge: Discuss Directions

(*Book B, Teacher Edition*, page 28)

See suggestions for teaching **Use Prior Knowledge** in the side column of the *Teacher Edition*, page 28.

Option A Before class, make four signs large enough to be read across the room. Write one direction word (*north, south, east,* or *west*) on each sign. Figure out which wall in your classroom is north and place the *north* sign on that wall about eye-level. Use the other signs later. Another approach is to tape arrows on the floor indicating directions.

Use a classroom map or a transparency of the United States. This activity will help students understand that they can figure out all four directions if they know one.

> ***Say:*** *There are four main directions on a map.* Point to the top of the map. ***Ask:*** *What direction is this?* Allow time for students to answer (north). ***Ask:*** *What direction is* opposite *of north?* If students don't understand *opposite,* point to the ceiling. ***Ask:*** *What is opposite the ceiling?* (Students will point to or ***say:*** *floor*) *Now what direction is* opposite *of north?* (south) *What direction is to the right/left of north?* (west/east)

Direct students to page 28.

> ***Say:*** *We are going to discuss directions. Point to the words "Discuss Directions" in your books. Point to the map. Is Arizona the most important state on this map?* (no) *What state does this map focus on?* (Texas) *Can you point to the compass rose (direction key) on the map?* (Circulate and monitor for comprehension.) Have a volunteer copy the direction key on the board. ***Ask:*** *What do the different letters mean?* Write the words on the direction key as students identify them.

Ask questions from Exercise 1. a–d one at a time. Allow volunteers to answer.

Divide the class into three groups.

> ***Ask:*** *Who can find the north side of this room?* Point out the sign you posted earlier if needed. Distribute one of the remaining direction signs to each group. ***Say:*** *Look at your direction.* Point to a group. ***Say:*** *Show your sign to the class and read it aloud together.* Repeat with other groups. ***Say:*** *Talk with your group and decide where your direction belongs in the room. Then pick a volunteer to put it up.*

When all the signs are up, have each group explain to the class how they figured out where their sign belonged.

Students can complete Exercise 2 in class or for homework. Collect their maps into a classroom "atlas."

4. Build Background: Antarctica (*Book B, Teacher Edition*, page 29)

Follow the directions for **1. Use a Map** on the side column in the *Teacher Edition*, page 29.

Have students look at the two maps on page 29. Ask factual questions about the maps, and then move to higher-order skill questions. Have a globe handy to view the South Pole, clarify directions, and help visual learners conceptualize the relationship between the two maps.

> ***Say:*** *Look at the big map. Is this a map of Antarctica?* (yes) *Does Antarctica touch countries on other continents?* (no) *What surrounds Antarctica?* (water, oceans) *Can you name the oceans?* (Indian Ocean, South Pacific Ocean, South Atlantic Ocean) *What countries are near Antarctica?* (Argentina, Chile, South Africa, Australia, New Zealand) *Now look at the small map. What do you see?* (North and South Poles, North and South America) *Is Antarctica the North Pole or the South Pole?* (South Pole) If student can't decide, ***say:*** *Look at the oceans around Antarctica again. Can you find a hint about where they are?* (*South* Pacific Ocean, *South* Atlantic Ocean, *South* Pole)

Read the paragraph *Antarctica* aloud.

> ***Ask:*** *Is it usually freezing cold on Antarctica?* (yes) *Is Antarctica an iceberg or a continent?* (continent) *Why do you think scientists in Antarctica live and study in underground buildings?* (sample answers: safety from the cold; equipment is protected from freezing) *Why do they go outside sometimes?* (sample answers: to do research, take pictures, observe wildlife, recreation, etc.) *Would you like to be a scientist there? Why or why not?* (sample answers: Yes. It would be exciting.)

TIP In South America, students are taught that there are six continents. North and South America are considered one continent.

Have a volunteer read the **Content Connection** box on the student page aloud. Ask questions from **2. Content Connection** on the side column of the *Teacher Edition* to get students to make predictions about the reading selection.

Use the suggestion on the bottom of the *Teacher Edition* page under **Content Connection: Social Studies.**

5. Build Vocabulary: Identify Words About Ships

(*Book B, Teacher Edition*, page 29)

Follow the suggestions in the *Teacher Edition* under **Identify Words About Ships,** including **1. Use experiences, 2. Use graphic features to locate information,** and **3. Reading selection vocabulary.**

Option A Teach vocabulary. Direct students to the graphic.

> ***Ask:*** *What do you see in this picture?* (ship, boat) Point to the word *sails.* ***Ask:*** *Who can read this word?* Allow a volunteer to pronounce it. ***Ask:*** *Does the ship have one sail?* (no) *Does it have many sails?* (yes) *One part of the ship is under the water. Is that the stern or the rudder?* (rudder) Point down to the floor. ***Say:*** *One part of a ship is like the floor. You can stand on it. What is the floor of a ship called?* (deck) Point to the word *bow.* ***Say:*** *This is the* bow. *Is the bow in the front or the back of a ship?* (front) *What is the back of a ship called?* (stern)

Bring in pictures of various ships or boats or have students print them from the Internet or draw their own. They can practice the vocabulary by labeling the parts. Point out that, in general, boats are small and ships are large. Have them describe their ships in small groups.

Option B Read or ask volunteers to read **Identify Words About Ships** aloud. Model completing the first sentence on the board.

> ***Write:*** *1. The front of a ship is the _____.* ***Say:*** *Who can read and complete this sentence?*

After a student answers correctly, give him or her the chalk to write the answer on the line.

Direct students to copy and complete sentences 1–5 in their Personal Dictionaries. Work with newcomers and beginning students to provide extra support as they work through the exercise.

Remember to have students complete the *Activity Book* assignment on page 17. They can work in small groups or do it for homework.

Follow the directions for **Learning Styles: Kinesthetic.**

Have students record new words in their Personal Dictionary in the *Teacher Resource Book,* page 63, or on the **Word Study and Spelling** chart in the *Student Handbook,* page 49.

See additional teaching suggestions for **Build Vocabulary** under **Multi-Level Options** on page 28.

If a computer lab is available, assign groups or individuals vocabulary reinforcement and practice activities on the *Student CD-ROM.*

6. Preview Text Structure: Historical Narrative

(*Book B, Teacher Edition,* page 30)

This is the first *narrative* reading selection in *Book B,* so be sure your students are familiar with the term. Write *historical narrative* on the board.

> ***Ask:*** Narrative. *What is a narrative? Does anyone know another word for narrative?* If no one can answer, ***say:*** *A narrative is a story of what happened. A narrative can be fiction or nonfiction (made up or true). Look at the top of page 30. Read the title in red along with me. Historical Narrative.*

Do a teacher think-aloud.

> ***Say:*** *I wonder if a historical narrative is fiction or nonfiction? Well, I know* historical *comes from* history. *History is real events, so an historical narrative must be about real events, so it's nonfiction. It's a story about something that really happened. Who agrees?*

Have students read the first column of **Historical Narrative** silently. To examine the chart, follow the suggestion on the side column of the *Teacher Edition* on page 30.

Ask students to write additional *wh-* questions for the graphic organizer.

> ***Say:*** *Look at the chart. What* wh- *word do you see next to "Events"?* (what [happened?]) *What* wh- *word do you see for dates?* (when [events happened in history]) *What* wh- *word asks about characters?* (who) *What* wh- *words ask about setting?* (where or what). *Work with a partner. Write one* wh- *question that asks about characters* (Who is the narrative about? Who is in the narrative?) *and one* wh- *question that asks about setting* (Where does the story take place? What does the place look like?).

Give students three or four minutes to write their questions. Then have volunteers share them with the class and tell them these questions will help them as they read the historical narrative.

If a computer lab is available, assign groups or individuals reinforcement and practice activities on the *Student CD-ROM.*

7. Reading Strategy: Predict (*Book B, Teacher Edition,* page 30)

Use the suggestions in 1. Share experiences in the *Teacher Edition* to explain what *predict* means. Try out suggestions from **Multi-Level Options** on the bottom of the *Teacher Edition,* page 30.

Option A

> ***Say:*** *The reading strategy for this chapter is* predict. Predict *is part of the word* prediction. Predict *is a verb, something you do.* Prediction *is a noun, a thing. What does* prediction *mean?* Students may know that a prediction is a guess. If not, ***say:*** *A prediction is a guess, a guess about what will happen.*
>
> *For example, people try to predict the weather. What will the weather be tomorrow? Will it be nice? Will it rain?* (Try to add a humorous or silly prediction; e.g. in hot climates ***ask:*** *Will it snow?* In cold climates: *Will it be hot?*)
>
> Then ***ask:*** *Are predictions always right?* (no) *Well, how can we make good predictions? Let's look at the chart on the bottom of page 30.*
>
> *Read the first box with me: Use clues. What's a clue?* If students can't answer, ***say:*** *a clue is a hint or a small bit of information. Clues help you make predictions. How can you predict rain? You look at the sky. Is it dark? That's a clue. Do you see clouds? That's another clue. Do you hear thunder? Another clue. Clues help you predict.*
>
> *Now look at the next box. Read with me: Clues are hints from what you read.*
>
> *Read the next box with me: Change predictions. Will a volunteer read why you might change your prediction?* Pick a volunteer to read the reason aloud.

Ask a volunteer to read aloud the paragraph above the chart as the class follows along. Check for comprehension.

Ask: Will you make predictions as you read Antarctic Adventure? (yes) *Can predicting or guessing make you a more active reader?* (yes)

Option B Do this activity *before* the **Reading Strategy** questions 1–4 on page 30.

Bring in two or three stories from a school or local community newspaper. Make sure the stories are at appropriate levels and content for your students. Cut out the headlines and photos, put them on transparencies, and show them one at a time.

Say: This is a headline, or title, of a news story. Read the headline with me and look at the picture(s). Read the headline aloud. *Say: Think about the headline and the picture. What do they tell you about the story? Who can make a prediction about the story?*

Allow students to make predictions. Ask them what information, or clues, helped them make their predictions.

Repeat the activity with other headlines if desired.

Read Exercise question 1.

Say: In a minute we will turn the page and see a picture of a ship. The ship's name is the Endurance. *You will listen to a small part of* Antarctic Adventure. *Read along with the audio. After you listen, think about what will happen to the ship next. Then make a prediction.*

Allow students time to find the correct page, look at the photograph, and find the numbered paragraphs. As a reminder, ask students the name of the ship in the photograph (the *Endurance*). Then play the audio of paragraphs 3 and 4 as students read along.

Ask for predictions, and write them on the board.

Say: Now listen to paragraph 5 and let's find out if the predictions are correct. Play the audio as students follow along. *Ask: Are the predictions correct? Did you use clues from the story* (the crackling sound) *and your prior knowledge* (boats with holes can sink) *to make your prediction? Continue predicting as we read the selection.*

Use the *Student CD-ROM* for additional practice with this reading strategy.

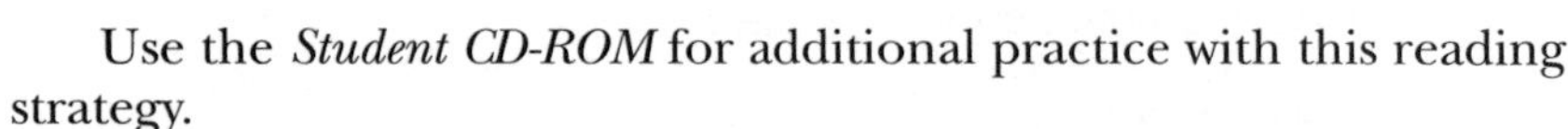

C. Reading Selection

(*Book B, Teacher Edition,* pages 31–35)

➤ Go to: *Book B, Teacher Edition,* Unit 1, Chapter 3, page 31

1. Reading Selection Materials (*Book B, Teacher Edition,* page 31)

Have the audio and Transparency #17 or the Reading Summary for Unit 1, Chapter 3 available.

2. Preview the Selection *(Book B, Teacher Edition,* page 31)

Follow suggestions to **1. Use a graphic organizer** (a KWL Chart is in the *Book B Teacher Resource Book* on page 42 and on Transparency #8) and **2. Connect** to prepare for the reading in the *Teacher Edition,* page 31.

Option A

> ***Say:*** *Let's look at page 31. Is the reading called* Antarctic Adventure? (yes) *Who wrote* Antarctic Adventure? (Meredith Cooper) *What kind of reading is it?* (historical narrative) *What is a narrative?* (a story; description of events) *Is it a true story?* (yes) *How do you know?* (historical) *Are we reading the whole book?* (no) *What are we reading?* (an excerpt)

Use the art in this section to talk about the reading selection and its connection to the unit theme, *Challenges.* Compare the landscape in this photo with the landscape in "Hatchet" on page 17.

Point to the picture.

> ***Say:*** *This is a landscape of the Antarctic. Landscapes are pictures of land or the setting. Are there any people or animals in this picture?* (no) *Do you see any trees or plants?* (no) *How does the land look?* (sample answers: flat, cold, white, in pieces) *What are the main colors?* (white, blue, grey) *How does the photo make you feel?* (sample answers: cold, lonely, scared, etc.)
>
> *We saw another landscape photograph in the story* Hatchet. *Look back at the photograph on page 17. Some things are similar in these photos and some things are different. You are going to work with a partner to compare these two landscape photographs.*

To create the pairs, have students count off *A* or *B*.

> ***Say:*** *"A" students raise your hand. You are responsible for the* Hatchet *photograph on page 17.* Check to make sure that their books are opened to the correct page. ***Say:*** *"B" students raise your hand. You will describe the* Antarctic Adventure *photograph on page 31.* Check again.

Draw a big Venn diagram on the board or easel or use Transparency #1. Write "Hatchet" on one side and "Antarctic Adventure" on the other side.

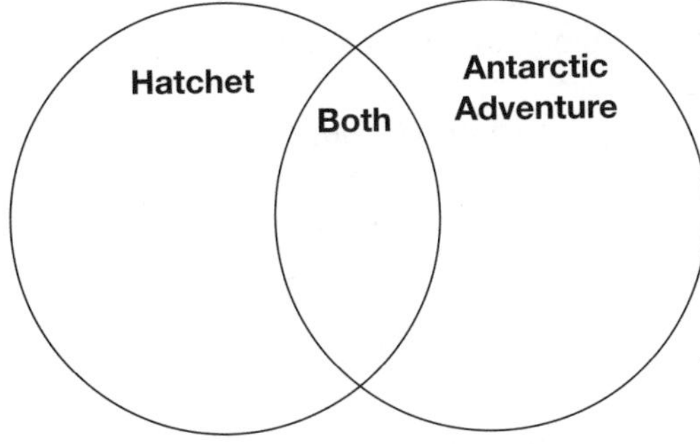

> ***Say:*** *Each pair shares one Venn diagram. "A" students write* Hatchet *on your side. "B" students write* Antarctic Adventure *on your side.*

Give each pair a blank copy of the Venn diagram (*Teacher Resource Book,* page 35) and have students copy the titles.

Demonstrate how to fill out the graphic organizer using the large Venn diagram.

> ***Ask:*** *"A" students, can you tell me one thing in your photo that's different than the other photo?* (trees, yellow sky, etc.) Have volunteers record one or two answers on the large diagram. Repeat for "B" students. (ice, blue sky, etc.) Then ***ask:*** *Can you tell me one thing that's the same in both pictures?* (water, sky, no people) To elicit the absence of things, ***ask:*** *Are there houses in the photos?* (no) ***Write:*** *no houses.* Have volunteers record one or two answers in the intersection of the large diagram.

Newcomers can draw pictures and use markers to compare colors in the two photos. Allow students a few minutes to complete their diagrams. Circulate and monitor the interactions. Combine several pairs to share their diagrams. Allow volunteers to add items to the large graphic organizer. Point out several of the best answers. Correct errors by asking how they could be improved. Post the final version on a bulletin board for later use.

Option B Ask students who are interested in technology to complete and share activities under **Content Connection.**

Students who are linguistic learners can do the activity about the Inuit language under **Learning Styles.**

3. Read the Selection (*Book B, Teacher Edition,* page 32)

The side column of the *Teacher Edition* has suggestions for teaching the reading selection, including **1. Use section headings, 2. Shared reading,** and **3. Make predictions.**

Help students' comprehension of the story by allowing them to read a summary of it in English or in their first language (*Teacher Resource Book,* pages 69–70) or do a read aloud with Transparency #17.

Before students read page 32, examine the text features on the page.

> ***Say:*** *Look at the top of page 32. Point to the* Prologue. *We read a prologue in* Hatchet. *What is a prologue for?* (provides background information, introduces characters, indicates time and place, etc.) *What other text features do you see?* (a photo, a photo caption, numbered paragraphs, bold-faced words and glosses, a Predict question). *What do you see in the photo?* (a ship, lots of ice, frozen waves, etc.) *Why isn't the photograph in color?* (sample answers: It's a very old picture. Color photographs didn't exist then.) *Does the* Endurance *look like a modern boat?* (no) *Why or why not?* (sample answer: It's wooden.) *Is this an easy trip for the* Endurance? (no) *Why not?* (sample answers: The water is frozen. There's ice all around it.)

Play or read the Prologue.

> ***Ask:*** *Did Ernest Shackleton fly to Antarctica?* (no) *When did he go to Antarctica?* (in 1914) *How did he travel?* (by ship, on the *Endurance*) *What did he want to do there?* (walk across the continent)

Have students listen to the audio of paragraphs 1–4, or read the paragraphs aloud as students follow along.

Say: I'm going to (play, read) the story again. This time, I want you to read aloud when you can. Later, I'm going to ask you some questions about the reading selection.

If necessary, play the audio and read along a third time. Ask the comprehension questions from the **Multi-Level Options.**

If the class already made a prediction about this part of reading for the **Reading Strategy** on page 30, don't repeat it. If the class didn't make a prediction then, do it now. Notice that the **Reading Strategy** boxes have small points that indicate which paragraph the question refers to.

4. Read the Selection (*Book B, Teacher Edition,* page 33)

Follow the suggestions in the *Teacher Edition* to **1. Understand terms, 2. Retell the order of events,** and do a **3. Paired reading.**

Option A Examine text features before reading page 33. Ask students to describe the photograph and the men in it.

After you play the audio or read aloud paragraphs 5 and 6, have students read the paragraphs again in pairs. Ask a volunteer to read the "Predict" box. Let the pairs formulate a prediction. Let volunteers share them with the class.

Then play the audio of paragraph 7.

Ask: Do you have to change your prediction because of new clues or was your prediction correct?

Play the audio or read aloud the rest of page 33.

Ask any remaining comprehension questions from **4. Multi-Level Options** on page 32.

Additional questions you can ask are: *Was ice crushing the ship?* (yes) *What happened when the rudder came off?* (sample answer: Water came into the ship.) *Where did the men go when they left the ship?* (onto the ice) *Was it a quiet night on the ice?* (no) *Why not?* (sample answers: The ice made noise and broke into pieces. The men had to move their tents three times.)

Follow directions for the **Spelling** activity on the bottom of the *Teacher Edition* page. Use it to start a two-column abbreviation chart for the classroom that students can add to and use as a reference guide. Assign the *Student CD-ROM* for additional practice with abbreviations. The *Activity Book* also contains additional **Spelling, Capitalization,** or **Punctuation** practice for each chapter in the **Writing** activities.

5. Read the Selection (*Book B, Teacher Edition,* pages 34–35)

Follow the directions on *Teacher Edition* page 34. Do the **1. Teacher read-aloud** and **2. Share feelings.** After students have completed paragraphs 17–22, do the **1. Shared reading** on page 35.

Watch the section of the *Staff Development Video* that demonstrates the reading strategy, Predict.

Option A Have pairs of students do a reciprocal reading using the reading strategy, Predict.

Say: We are going to read the rest of the story with partners. You and your partner will take turns reading and predicting.

First, your partner reads one paragraph aloud.

Listen to your partner read. Then you make a prediction or ask a question about the next paragraph. Then it's your turn to read one paragraph. What do you think your partner does? (listens, predicts, or asks a question) *That's right. Your partner listens to you read and predicts or asks a question about the next paragraph.*

Say: *I'm going to show you how to read and predict with a partner. First, let's open to page 34. Point to paragraph 10.* (Allow students time to find the place.) *Can I have a volunteer to be my partner?* Sit with the student. Be sure you are facing each other and gesture between you. ***Say:*** *First, we sit face to face. Second,* (student) *will read paragraph 10 and stop. Just read one paragraph. I will listen carefully. Then I will make a prediction or ask a question. Ready? Go ahead,* (student)!

Have the student read paragraph 10.

Then ***say:*** *First, I think about the paragraph. Hmm. Here's my prediction: I don't think they will get to land 312 miles away.*

What do we do next? (you read; (student) listens). *Good! I will read paragraph 11 and stop. What will* (student) *do then?* (predict or ask a question) *That's right.*

Read the paragraph aloud. Let your partner predict or ask a question.

Say: *That's a good prediction/question.* Turn to the class. *Do you know how to read with your partner now? Any questions?*

Move your chairs so you face your partner. Gesture getting up, moving chairs, and facing each other. Once everyone is settled, ***ask:*** *Raise your hand if you're the first reader. Start with paragraph 12. Okay, you can start now.*

Assist any students who need help after the others begin.

Option B Prepare a Cloze exercise using the Reading Summary of "Antarctic Adventure" in the *Teacher Resource Book,* page 69. Using a copy of the summary, cover each word that you want your students to focus on. Some examples of words to cover include proper nouns; numbers: 1914, 278, 312, three, five, two, etc.; plurals: men, miles, days, months, etc.; or irregular verbs: is, get, begin, stuck, etc. Distribute a copy of the Cloze to each student. Play the audio of the summary or read it aloud two or three times. Pause after each blank to give students time to write the answer. Provide a word box of missing words, if needed.

Allow students to correct their own work by showing the complete reading summary on Transparency #17.

Option C After students read, ask comprehension questions from **Multi-Level Options** on the bottom of *Teacher Edition* page 34.

Follow directions for the **Capitalization** activity on the bottom of *Teacher Edition* page 34.

Evaluate Your Reading Strategy, on the bottom of page 35, helps students think about how well they use the reading strategy in the chapter.

Copy the boxed reading evaluation statement ("I use clues from the story. . . .) on the board or a transparency.

> ***Ask:*** *What reading strategy did you practice in this chapter?* (Predict) *Predict, that's right. You have practiced an important reading strategy. Now you can decide how well you have done.*

Have the class read the statement aloud together from the board or the transparency.

> ***Say:*** *Think about the statement. Do you use clues to make predictions? Is this statement true for you? Raise your hand if this statement is true for you.* Pause and look around. ***Say:*** *Very good. Now let's remember to predict as we read.*

6. About the Author (*Book B, Teacher Edition,* page 35)

Read **1. Explain Author's Background** on the side column of the *Teacher Edition.*

> ***Ask:*** *Is Meredith Hooper an American author?* (no) *Where is she from?* (Australia) *What continent does she love to visit?* (Antarctica) *What does she write about?* (natural history, the natural world, man's place in the world)

Ask **2. Interpret the facts** question.

> ***Say:*** *Now you are going to read more about Ms. Hooper in your books. Work in groups of four students. Move your chairs into a circle.* Gesture and demonstrate, if needed. After the students are correctly settled, ***say:*** *Now figure out what direction you are sitting in. Are you near the east? The north? The south or west? How can you tell?* If students don't remember, point to the direction signs they put up during **Use Prior Knowledge.** ***Say:*** *Yes. You can look at the direction signs.* Take some time and decide who is sitting in the north, the south, the east, and the west. The purpose of this activity is to review directions and use the information to choose a group leader. Choose a direction. ***Say:*** *Will students sitting in the* (direction) *raise their hands?* When one member of each group has responded ***say:*** *You will be the group leader.*

Direct leaders to choose students to read the paragraph and discuss the questions that follow it. Then ask leaders to say if their group thinks Hooper wrote to inform, entertain, or influence. (inform)

Option A Have students listen to the story on the *Audio Program* (CD 1, Track 4).

7. Across Selections
(*Book B, Teacher Edition,* page 35)

Follow the directions for **Compare and Contrast** on the side column of the *Teacher Edition,* page 35. Students can add words, captions, or sentences to the Venn diagram they did for **Preview the Selection.** If they didn't do that activity, they can create new Venn diagrams. Advanced students can write to compare and contrast the two readings.

Do the **Capitalization** activity.

D. Beyond the Reading

(*Book B, Teacher Edition,* pages 36–39)

➤ Go to: *Book B, Teacher Edition* Unit 1, Chapter 3, page 36

1. Reading Comprehension: Question-Answer Relationships (QAR) (*Book B, Teacher Edition,* page 36)

Have students record any written answers in their Reading Logs.

a. **"Right There"** Questions: Divide the class into four groups. Assign each group one question. Give them three minutes to recall the factual information and write an answer in a complete sentence. Have two members of each group present the question and answer to the class.

b. **"Think and Search"** Questions: Have the four groups discuss these questions for five minutes. Then combine them into two groups and have them share their responses. Circulate and monitor the discussions.

c. **"Author and You"** Questions: Read the questions aloud. If your students have trouble with the level, ask these additional clarifying questions:

8. Understand Character Traits

Ask: *Do the men follow Shackleton?* (yes) *Does he know how to take care of problems?* (yes) *Is Shackleton a good or a bad leader?* (good) *How do you know that he cares about his men?* (sample answer: He goes back to rescue them from Elephant Island.)

9. Understand Plot

Ask: *Do you think the men were happy on Elephant Island?* (no) *Did the men have good food and nice homes there?* (no) *Was their life on Elephant Island hard or easy?* (hard) *What did they miss from home?* (sample answers: their families, warm houses, lots of food)

10. Use Visual Elements

Ask: *Did the photographs show interesting parts of the story?* (yes) *What did you learn from the photos?* (sample answer: what ice floes really look like) *Were all the photographs taken during the trip?* (no) *Which photographs did you like best?* (sample answer: the photograph of the *Endurance*) *Why did you like it?* (sample answer: I wanted to know what the ship looked like.) *What parts of the story do the photographs tell about?* (sample answer: how the *Endurance* looked as it pushed through the ice)

11. "On Your Own" Questions: Express Your Opinion

Read the question aloud. If your students have trouble with the level ask these additional clarifying questions.

Ask: *Where would you go?* (sample answer: the Colorado River) *What would you do there?* (ride down the river) *What is the challenge there?* (fast rapids, the white water, waterfalls)

For additional skill work, students can use **Spell Words with the Suffix *-ly*** in the *Activity Book,* page 18.

If a computer lab is available, assign groups or individuals reinforcement and practice activities on the *Student CD-ROM.*

2. Build Reading Fluency: Rapid Word Recognition

(*Book B, Teacher Edition,* page 36)

See suggestions for teaching in the side column of the *Teacher Edition,* page 36, or watch the section of the *Staff Development Video* that demonstrates rapid word recognition.

Option A Make seven large flash cards, each with one word from the grid. Slowly hold up each card in turn. ***Ask:*** *What's this word?* Let the whole class answer. Then ask a volunteer to define it or to use it in a sentence. Repeat with all the words in the pile one time. Then shuffle the pack. Show the cards again, but flash the words for a shorter time. Shuffle the pack once more and just flash each word briefly. Then follow the activity in the student book.

Option B On the board, ***write:*** *deck, each, fight, huge, ice, pack, stuck.* ***Say:*** *Read these words with me.* Point to each word first in order, then out of order, as students say them aloud.

> ***Say:*** *Find the word grid on page 36. Let's read the first column together: fight, stuck, pack, ice, huge. You have one minute to read as many words aloud as you can. When I say* time *everyone stops. Everybody ready? One, two, three, start.* Use a stopwatch. After one minute, ***say:*** *Time. Everybody stop reading. Count the words you read, and record that number in your Reading Fluency Chart.* (*Book B, Teacher Resource Book,* page 116)

3. Listen, Speak, Interact: Retell Order of Events

(*Book B, Teacher Edition,* page 37)

See suggestions for teaching in the side column of the *Teacher Edition,* page 37.

Option A Work with students to make a classroom reference chart labeled *Time Words.* Start with time words from "Antarctic Adventure" (*in the beginning, end; three times; on Saturday, morning, one evening; five months later; after seven days; three months*). Add new words as they discover them in other content materials.

Option B Make a timeline of Shackleton's trip using a wall in the classroom or a nearby hallway. Have students work in groups of three. Each group can concentrate on one page or one section of "Antarctic Adventure." One student records time words, another records chunks of the story, and the third student draws pictures to show the events. Have each group present its material orally as the class verifies the correct order. Then affix text and illustrations to their points in the timeline.

Students can use the checklist to **Edit a Historical Narrative** in the *Activity Book,* page 23, to revise their work. Or for a more extensive revision, they can use the **Editor's Checklist** in the *Student Handbook,* pages 10–11.

4. Elements of Literature: Identify Personification

(*Book B, Teacher Edition,* page 37)

Follow the directions on the side column of the *Teacher Edition,* page 37, for **2. Locate derivation** and **3. Use personal experience.**

See additional teaching suggestions for **Elements of Literature** under **Multi-Level Options** on the bottom of *Teacher Edition* page 36.

Watch the section of the *Staff Development Video* that discusses personification.

Option A On the board, ***write:*** *personification.*

> ***Say:*** *Personification. Repeat that word.* Pause for a response. ***Say:*** *Say it again. Personification.* Pause for a response. ***Say:*** *What root word do you see in* personification? (person) Draw a box around *person.*
>
> ***Say:*** *Authors use personification to make stories more lively and interesting. Personification makes an object, a thing, act like a person or do things a person does. In* Antarctic Adventure *there's Shackleton and his men. What's the next most important thing in the story?* (the *Endurance,* a boat) *Is the* Endurance *a person?* (no) *But Shackleton says, "She's going, boys!" Does the* Endurance *have a voice?* (no) *But the author says: "The* Endurance *groaned" just like a person! What does a groan sound like?* Let students make the noises, or make a loud groaning sound yourself if they're reluctant. ***Ask:*** *Can a boat groan?* (sample answer: the deck creaks)
>
> Find two other examples of personification in paragraphs 10 (the ice floes groaned) and 13 (the ice was friendly). Record them in your Reading Log.

Tell students to work with a partner to complete page 19 in the *Activity Book.* Compile their work into a classroom chart labeled "Personifications." Allow students to refer to the chart when they write their historical narratives for **From Reading to Writing** on page 39.

Follow the directions for the **Home Connection** and **Learning Styles: Visual** activities on the bottom of *Teacher Edition* page 37. Encourage learners to select one activity to complete for a long-term homework assignment.

Follow the directions for **Compare and Contrast** on the side column of the *Teacher Edition,* page 35.

If a computer lab is available, assign groups or individuals reinforcement and practice activities on the *Student CD-ROM.*

5. 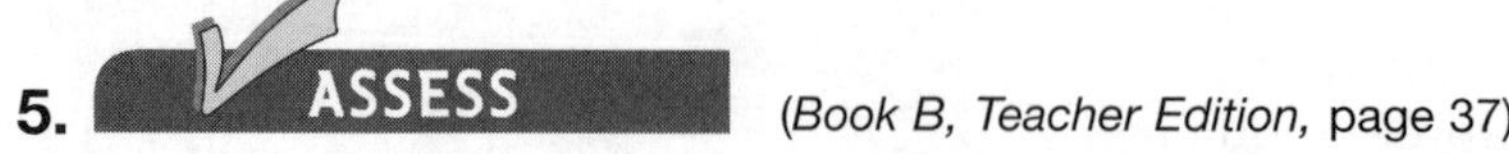

(*Book B, Teacher Edition,* page 37)

Have students write their sentences on three strips of paper, mix the sentences up, and give them to a partner. The partner should rearrange the sentences in correct order. If the order is incorrect, help the writer to revise the time words. Write out the directions for this **Assess** on the board or on a transparency, so students can refer back to it as they check their work.

6. Word Study: Use Adverbs (*Book B, Teacher Edition,* page 38)

Follow the directions on the side column of the *Teacher Edition,* page 38, for a Roundtable.

Option A After you write each sentence below on the board, exaggerate the final adverb, so students begin to focus on it.

> ***Write,*** *then* ***say:*** *The ship sailed slowly.* ***Ask:*** *How did the ship sail?* (slowly) Circle *slowly.* ***Write:*** *Shackleton yelled loudly.* ***Ask:*** *How did he yell?* (loudly) Circle *loudly.* Point to the circled words. ***Ask:*** *What letters do both words end with?* (with *-ly*) *When you describe how something happens, you can use a word ending in* -ly. *Words that end in* -ly *are called adverbs. What are they called?* (adverbs)
>
> *Turn to page 34. Look at paragraph 13. Read the first sentence to yourselves. Tell me* how *the ice was.* (friendly) *Look at paragraph 15. Tell me* how *Shackleton shouted.* (sadly) *Find two more* -ly *adverbs in paragraphs 15 and 16.* (slowly, lonely)

Then have students record the adverbs in their Personal Dictionaries. Students who are able should write an original sentence using an *-ly* adverb. For additional practice with adverbs, have students complete the *Activity Book,* page 20. Have students record new words on the **Word Study** and **Spelling** chart in the *Student Handbook,* page 49.

If a computer lab is available, assign groups or individuals reinforcement and practice activities on using adverbs on the *Student CD-ROM.*

7. Grammar Focus: Use *And* to Join Words and Sentences

(*Book B, Teacher Edition,* page 38)

Follow suggestions in the *Teacher Edition* for Modeling. Write the two sentences on one line. Write the sentence joined with *and* underneath.

> ***Ask:*** *Do these sentences have the same meaning?* (yes) *How are they different?* (sample answers: The second line is shorter. No words repeat.) Additional examples: The ship is small. The ship is brown. The trip is long. The trip is dangerous.

Divide the class into small groups. Give each group four sheets of paper. Have each group write additional pairs of simple sentences with repeating nouns, verbs, adjectives, and adverbs, one pair to each sheet. Hang the papers around the room and have groups circulate, combining the sentences using *and.* Tell them they can use any vocabulary from their Personal Dictionaries. Have volunteers read the completed sheets aloud.

Refer students to **Grammar Focus** in the *Activity Book,* page 21. Work with newcomers and beginning students to complete Exercise A. At the same time, intermediate and advanced students can do Exercise B. Then have students work in small, multi-level groups to review both exercises. Advanced students can also refer to the *Student Handbook,* page 44, for more information about adverbs.

If a computer lab is available, assign groups or individuals reinforcement and practice activities on the *Student CD-ROM.* Use *More Grammar Practice 1* and *2* for more support for this grammatical structure.

8. From Reading to Writing (*Book B, Teacher Edition,* page 39)

Follow the directions on the side column of the *Teacher Edition,* page 39, including additional teaching suggestions under **Multi-Level Options** on the bottom of the *Teacher Edition,* page 38.

Option A Have students read the paragraph and the seven directions silently.

> On the board, ***write:*** *Historical Narrative* ***Say:*** *You are going to write a historical narrative about a person and a challenge they faced. Think about a person who faced a challenge. It can be a famous person like Shackleton. Or it can be someone you know.*
>
> ***Say:*** *You will use the* text structure *of a historical narrative.* ***Write:*** *Text structure.* ***Say:*** *Who remembers the features of a historical narrative?* (events, dates, characters, setting) Refer students to page 30, if needed. ***Say:*** *That's right. You describe* what happened *and* who *did it. You describe* when *and* where *it happened, too.*

In a column on the board, write: *Who? When? Where?* Encourage intermediate and advanced students to write complete answers to each question. Allow newcomers and beginning students to draw pictures or find them on the Internet.

> ***Say:*** *Write down the person's name. Or raise your hand and tell me the name. I will write it down.*

Display Transparency #16: Chronological Order, also found in the *Teacher Resource Book,* page 50.

> ***Say:*** *Use this chart for a historical narrative. We will practice by writing about* Antarctic Adventure. Record answers on the transparency. ***Ask:*** *First,* who *is this story about? What is the* character's name? (Ernest Shackleton) When *did the story happen? What* dates *are in the story?* (1914 to 1915) Where *does the story happen? What is the* setting? (South Pole, Antarctica, Elephant Island)

Then go to the board for a brainstorm.

> ***Say:*** *Now let's think about the events in the story. What important things happened to Shackleton and his men?*
>
> List events as students call them out. Help students combine ideas that are related with *and.* Have students decide the four most important events. ***Say:*** *Now, put these events in order. What happened first?* Number the events. Then copy them on the transparency.

Distribute copies of the graphic organizer, Chronological Order, to each student and let them begin work. Circulate and assist as needed. Have less fluent students dictate their stories as you write them. Then have students practice reading their stories to partners and create a timeline to illustrate the narratives. If they made a timeline for **Listen, Speak, Interact: Retell Order of Events,** encourage them to review it before they begin work. Remind students to use pages 10–11, 15, 44–45, and 51 in the *Student Handbook* to support their writing.

9. Across Content Areas: Social Studies

(*Book B, Teacher Edition,* page 39)

Follow the directions on the side column of the *Teacher Edition,* page 39.

Option A To learn the names of the continents, teach students "All the continents in the world," sung to "He's got the whole world in his hand." See the *Staff Development Video* for a demonstration.

Asia's the first continent in the world,
Yes, Asia's the first continent in the world,
Oh, Asia's the first continent in the world, continent in the world.

Africa's the second continent in the world . . .
North 'merica's the third continent in the world . . .
. . .
Antarctica's the seventh continent in the world. . . .

Have students work in pairs to complete the exercise, Take Notes, in the *Activity Book* on page 24. Then combine pairs to compare the information they recorded on their note cards.

10. Reteach and Reassess (*Book B, Teacher Edition,* page 39)

Follow the directions to review **Text Structure** and **Reading Strategy** with your class. After students have written or drawn, collect the materials in a class book. Have students choose a title for their book and create a table of contents. Keep the book in the class library and let students add to it throughout the year.

For **Reassess,** students can write or draw their prediction and share it with the class.

11. Assessment Program

A multiple-choice chapter quiz can be found in the *Assessment Program* on pages 11–12. The quiz questions can be re-sequenced by using the *ExamView® Pro* test generator on the *Assessment CD-ROM.* Questions may also be added, revised, or deleted. Before assigning the quiz, review each section with the class. The quiz may be given in sections, rather than all in one sitting.

If needed, show students how to answer each section by providing an example.

> ***Say:*** *Part A asks about vocabulary. Point to question 1. Read the sentence like this: The BLANK is the back of a ship. Then look at the words under the sentence.* Let volunteers read answers a.–d. ***Say:*** *Read the sentence again and say a. Sail. The* sail *is the back of a ship. Is that right?* (no) *Try the next word. The* stern *is the back of a ship. Is that right?* (yes) *Yes, it is. Underline* stern. *Answer vocabulary questions 1–6.*
>
> ***Say:*** *Part B asks about text structure and literature focus. Point to the box on page 11. Read it along with me.* Read the boxed

reading aloud. If needed, allow students to reread with a partner. Then have students answer questions 7–13.

Say: *Part C asks about the chapter's reading strategy. In Part C find the* best *answer to complete the sentence. Point to question 14.* Check that everyone is there. ***Read:*** *Predicting is when the reader. . . . Now point to a. Say to yourself: Predicting is when the reader a. reads the whole story without stopping. Is that right? Is predicting reading the whole story?* (no) *So read the next answer.*

Now point to b. Say to yourself: Predicting is when the reader b. describes the setting of the story. Is predicting describing the setting? (no) *No it isn't. So keep looking.*

Now point to c. Would a volunteer like to model c? Let students model c. and d. (the right answer) Then have students answer questions 15 and 16.

Continue explaining how to do the questions for Part D. Read the writing prompt for Part E. Allow Newcomers and Beginning students to draw and label their writing.

E. Apply and Expand

(*Book B, Teacher Edition,* pages 72–77)

1. Listening/Speaking Workshop: Make a Speech: News Report (*Book B, Teacher Edition,* pages 72–73)

Follow the directions on the side column of the *Teacher Edition,* page 72, including additional teaching suggestions under **Multi-Level Options** on the bottom of the *Teacher Edition,* page 72.

Option A To prepare students for presenting their news reports, tape a sample news report from a local or national news program or tell students to watch the news for several evenings. News stories about heroes, celebrities involved in social or charitable work, or come-from-behind sports stories are especially suitable.

Give students copies of the **Sunshine Organizer** from the *Teacher Resource Book,* page 40. Use Transparency #6 as you work through the following preparation.

Before viewing your tape, ***say:*** *In this unit, you read about challenges. For our Listening/Speaking Workshop you are going to make a speech about a challenge. The speech is a news report. To get ready, we are going to watch a news report together. You will see the report three times. After the first viewing, we'll talk about the topic of the report. We'll ask, What was this report about? Then we will fill out the Sunshine Organizer. Where will we write the topic?* (on the line in the middle) *Right. After the second viewing, we'll talk about the person and the setting. Where will we write that information?* (in Who? and Where?) *After the third viewing, we'll talk about the challenge. We'll ask, What challenge did the person face?*

Any questions? (pause and answer, if needed) *Everyone ready? Let's go!*

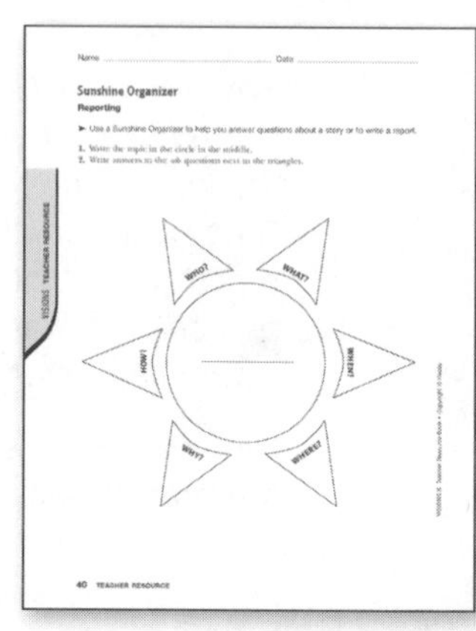

Option B Review **How to Give an Oral Presentation** in the *Student Handbook* on page 1, if needed. As students work on their visuals, have them use the **Viewing Checklist** in the *Student Handbook* on page 4. Encourage visual learners to organize and create a classroom "news set" as described in **Learning Styles** on the bottom of the *Teacher Edition,* page 73.

Remind listeners to use the **Active Listening Checklist** in the *Student Handbook,* page 3, so they can give useful feedback. After speaking, remind students to listen to the feedback and reflect on their presentation, using the **Speaking Checklist** in the *Student Handbook,* page 2. Some students may be ready to expand their checklists to include additional refinements or to add their own criteria.

Option C Allow students to invite special guests, such as parents or siblings, to the school to see the presentations.

Option D If possible, videotape the presentations. Have students view their own presentations privately and critique them using the **Speaking Checklist.**

(*Book B, Teacher Edition,* page 73)

Have students record their sentences in their Reading Logs and refer to their goals the next time they do an oral presentation.

Portfolio (*Book B, Teacher Edition,* page 73)

Provide each student with a large envelope or folder in which to file his or her best work. The portfolios should be kept together and filed alphabetically in a safe, but accessible area of the classroom. Allow students to decorate the portfolios. Use the **Portfolio Assessment** (*Book B, Assessment Program,* page 115) to evaluate student progress.

2. Viewing Workshop (*Book B, Teacher Edition,* page 73)

Follow the directions on the side column of the *Teacher Edition,* page 73. Do the activity described in **Content Connection: Social Studies** on the bottom of that page.

Use the **Video Worksheet** in the *Teacher Resource Book,* page 173, to help students view the *CNN Video* for Unit 1.

Option A Create a Cloze exercise from the video script "Antarctic Survival" in the *Teacher Resource Book,* page 161. Select parts of the script with key review words, copy the speeches, and white out the words. Focus on words from the reading such as *continent, ice, journey,* and *ship.*

Option B Students can use context clues to learn new vocabulary. Distribute copies of the video script for "Antarctic Survival" in the *Teacher Resource Book,* page 161.

Divide the class into small groups. Assign groups two or three speeches to work with.

> **Say:** *Find at least two new words in the speeches. Underline the words and use context to figure out their meanings. Check the meaning using another reference aid, such as the* Heinle Newbury House Dictionary. *Then write a synonym or sentence for each word.*

Students should share their new words and meanings with another group or the class.

3. Writer's Workshop (*Book B, Teacher Edition,* pages 74–75)

Follow the teaching suggestions on the side columns of *Book B, Teacher Edition,* pages 74–75. **Multi-Level Options** on the bottom of that page provides additional ideas for teaching the **Writer's Workshop.**

Students can also review **The Writing Process** in the *Student Handbook* on pages 6–7.

Option A Teach the steps in **The Writing Process,** starting with gathering information and doing research.

First, gather information and do research. Tell students it is helpful to start the process by writing the *topic* at the top of the page.

> ***Say:*** *Let's use a topic from* Antarctic Adventure. ***Write:*** *Shackleton's challenge: rescue 22 men from Elephant Island.*
>
> ***Say:*** *First, brainstorm ideas about the topic. To brainstorm, write down* all *the words and ideas you think of. Don't stop to think and decide which ideas are useful yet. Just list ideas as you think of them. Look at the topic often as you brainstorm. Reviewing the topic keeps your mind on the subject. It also reminds you of the purpose of your writing. Later you will organize your ideas.*

Point out that it's normal to find that some ideas from a brainstorm don't fit into the narrative. They can be crossed off.

> ***Ask:*** *When you brainstorm, do you write careful, complete sentences?* (no) *Do you check spelling?* (no) *Do you list* all *the ideas about the topic?* (yes) *Right.*
>
> *Now read Shackleton's challenge: "rescue 22 men from Elephant Island."*
>
> *Raise your hand as soon as you have an idea about this challenge. I'll jot it on the board.* After you list each idea, ***say:*** *Good work.*

Next, organize ideas.

> ***Say:*** *The next step is to organize your ideas. You organize ideas by grouping similar ideas together. Use graphic organizers to help you. What kinds of graphic organizers help organize information?* (webs, cluster maps, timelines, and sunshine organizers)

Then, students should think about their *purpose* for writing and their audience.

> ***Say:*** *Read the topic again.* (Shackleton's challenge: rescue 22 men from Elephant Island.) *Is the purpose of this narrative to explain, persuade, or to entertain?* (explain) *Who is the audience?* (sample answer: teacher, classmates, parents)

Next, write a draft. Focus students' attention on the sections of a narrative, and show how to group ideas into sections.

> ***Say:*** *Now what are the three main sections of the story chart?* (Beginning, Middle, End) Allow students to look at the story chart on page 74, if needed.

Ask: What information is in the beginning? (opening, topic, characters, and setting) *Let's look at our list again. Let's put a* B *next to each idea that belongs in the* beginning.

Do a similar exercise for the Middle and End sections.

To teach students to refine their writing further, focus on the Middle section. If possible, put all Middle section items on a transparency in the order they were listed. Then ask students to put the events in order, writing a number for each item. Ask them to add some details, such as dates and description, and to use time words like *first, then,* and *next.*

To edit the draft, model using the **Peer Editing Checklist** in the *Student Handbook,* pages 12–13. Ask a volunteer to let the class use his or her first draft as the sample. Make a transparency of it.

> ***Say:*** *Open to page 12 in your* Student Handbook. *Look at the questions on the* ***Peer Editing Checklist. Ask:*** *What's the first thing a peer editor looks for?* (the title) *What's the next thing to look for?* (indented paragraphs) Continue asking verifying questions.

Then have students work in groups to review **Responding to Peers' Writing: EQS** on page 13.

Show the transparency of the sample first draft. Have the author (or another volunteer, if the author wants to be anonymous) read the draft aloud as the class follows along.

> ***Say:*** *Look at the* ***Peer Editing Checklist*** *on page 12. You are going to answer the questions by checking with your finger. Ready? Let's begin. Number 1. Is there a title? With your finger, check Yes or No.*

If there is a title, ask for and record phrases that students can use to praise authors. If there's no title, ask for and record helpful phrases that students can use to question or suggest what the author can do. Continue asking each question as students "check" answers with their fingers. For questions 6–8, students can say their answers aloud.

For Steps 4 and 5 of the **Writer's Workshop,** remind students to use the **Editor's Checklist** in the *Student Handbook* on pages 10 and 11. Also remind them to use the *Heinle Newbury House Dictionary* to check for correct spelling and meaning of words.

Students can share information about Unit 1 with their families through a letter and interview in English or in their first language. Have students take home the **School-Home Connection** in the *Teacher Resource Book,* pages 119–125. Have students share their interviews with a partner.

4. Projects (*Book B, Teacher Edition,* page 76)

Follow the teaching suggestions on the side column of the *Teacher Edition,* page 76. **Multi-Level Options** on the bottom of that page provides additional ideas for assisting students with **Projects.**

Option A For students who chose **Project 1: Create a Poster About Meeting Challenges,** teach about polls. Have students read the first paragraph silently. Then have a volunteer read #1 and ask comprehension questions that lead students to understand the task.

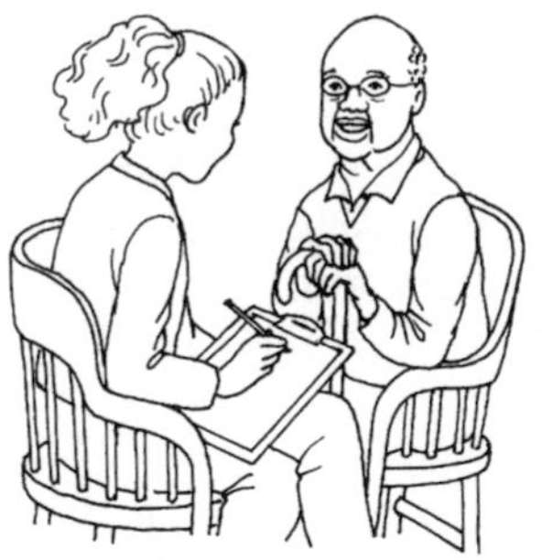

> ***Say:*** *Polls ask questions. What question does this poll ask?* (What are the three most important qualities to help people meet challenges?) *How many people will you ask?* (10) *Will you only ask*

people in this room? (no) *Will you ask young and old people?* (yes) *Will you ask people from different cultures?* (yes) *That's right. In a poll, you want to ask different kinds of people.*

Have a volunteer read #2.

Ask: *What will you write down for this poll?* (names, responses)

If needed, summarize and ***say:*** *A poll is a way to get information. In a poll, you ask different people to answer a question.*

Demonstrate to students how to record information from their poll on a two-column chart. Use Transparency #10.

Say: *Write the question in the top box.* In the top box, ***write:*** *What are the top three most important qualities that help meet challenges?*

Point to the left-hand column. Write as you ***say:*** *Number this column from one to ten. What information goes in the first column?* (names) Point to the right-hand column. ***Ask:*** *What information goes in the second column?* (answers; the important qualities)

Say: *Read the green chart on page 76.* Point to the first box on the transparency chart and record the answers. ***Ask:*** *What information from the green chart goes here?* (my mother) Point to the next box across. ***Ask:*** *What information goes here?* (1. intelligence, 2. courage, 3. keeps trying)

Have a volunteer model asking you the question and recording information on the transparency. For your answer, use one quality already recorded (intelligence, courage, or keeps trying) and add two new qualities such as *tries new solutions, is creative, finds good helpers.* Then have several pairs of volunteers model asking and recording information on the transparency.

Give students copies of the two-column chart.

Ask: *Where do you write the question?* (in the top box) *Write the question now. How many boxes do you number?* (10) *Write the numbers. Now, poll one person in this class. Write their response.*

Return to the student book, page 76, and have volunteers read #3–#5.

Say: *Get information for the poster from your poll.* Point to the data on the transparency. *What qualities are named most often?* Circle the top three. ***Say:*** *Use the top qualities you find in your poster.*

You can have students complete their polls around school or for homework. Students can report the results, either orally or by posting their survey charts.

Option B Teach students choosing **Project 2: Write a Magazine Article or a Web Article** how to take notes for their project. Use Transparency #24.

Model Transparency #24 Note-Taking. Do a teacher think-aloud.

Say: *Shackleton went to the Antarctic a long time ago. He lost his ship. Lots of other things were lost, too. But we saw pictures from the trip. My question is: How did Shackleton save all those pictures of his voyage?*

Point to where the question goes on the index card. Write it in the correct space.

Say: *Now where can I find an answer to this question?* After students respond, **say:** *Those are good places to find information.* If no one mentioned the CNN video, **say:** *In the Viewing Workshop, we saw a news report on "Antarctic Survival." Let's use the video script for our research.* Highlight Tornquist's second and fourth narrations. **Say:** *Read silently the paragraph that starts "80 years later." I'm going to summarize that paragraph on my index card.*

As the class reads, ***write:*** *150 photographs and film clips of Shackleton's journey to Antarctica are on display at the American Museum of Natural History. Frank Hurley took the pictures.*

Discuss your summary with the class.

Ask: *Did I copy the words exactly from the script?* (no) *Does the summary include important information from the script?* (yes) *Did I use my own words or Tornquist's words?* (own words)

Then **say:** *I also want to quote my source. That means I want to use some of Tornquist's words exactly. I want to quote her. Look at the next paragraph. Read it and decide what sentence would make an exciting quote.*

After the students choose an appropriate quote, show where to put it on the index card and how to enclose it in quotation marks. Tell students the Source page is a helpful record of where information is found. ***Write:*** *Cynthia Tornquist, CNN, New York.* CNN Video to accompany *Visions: Language, Literature, Content.* Videocassette. Heinle/Thomson and Turner Broadcasting System, Inc., an AOL Time Warner Company, 2004.

Then direct students to follow the remaining directions on page 76.

5. Further Reading (*Book B, Teacher Edition,* page 77)

Students can complete the exercises on page 77 using an additional title from the **Heinle Reading Library** on the theme of Challenges, such as *Treasure Island,* by Robert Louis Stevenson.

Have students record their answers in their Reading Logs. Give each student a copy from the *Teacher Resource Book,* page 64.

6. Assessment Program

Use the Unit 1 Test to assess student progress. The test can be found in the *Assessment Program,* pages 17–22. Read "The Audition" aloud with newcomers and beginning students. Before administering the unit test, review During the Test and Types of Test Questions with the class. These suggestions, part of **Test-Taking Tips,** can be found in the *Assessment Program* on pages 132–133 and in the *Student Handbook* on pages 55–56.

Try It Out

Teacher Activity: Compare with Own Experiences

Use a blank Venn diagram from the *Teacher Resource Book,* page 35, or Transparency #1. Think about your own learning-to-read experiences in the past (in English or in another language). Compare your experiences with the experiences of students you have or expect to have. Record similarities and differences in the diagram. Share your completed diagrams in small groups.

Teacher Reflections

Think about and discuss these questions with your colleagues.

1. What differences did you note? What circumstances might have caused these differences?
2. How can you use this activity with your students?
3. How does this activity relate to the standards you must meet?

 A. *Student Book*

The *Visions Basic Student Book* contains two types of chapters. The first type—Chapters A, B, C, and D—introduces phonics and phonemic awareness, basic literacy skills, and essential functional vocabulary. The second type—Chapters 1–10—continues building vocabulary, developing language skills, and phonics instruction in addition to reading and writing skill-building activities.

Each chapter in *Visions Basic* is organized around a theme of special relevance to, and appropriateness for, newcomers to English. Themes include critical information about the school, home, and community, as well as personal and cultural content to help students succeed in their new environment.

At this level, students are taught receptive language skills first, followed by productive language skills. Icons throughout the *Student Book* indicate which exercises focus on listening and reading (receptive), and which focus on pointing, speaking, and writing (productive). In *Visions Basic,* students learn to:

a. recognize simple vocabulary to communicate basic needs in social and academic settings;

b. learn the skills needed to decode words and identify sight words and cognates;

c. demonstrate comprehension of simple vocabulary with an appropriate action; and

d. apply the vocabulary initially through retelling information supported by pictures, acting out, labeling, and by the end of the book, through expository speaking and writing.

Content and academic language are introduced and practiced to enable beginning students to transition into *Visions A, B,* or *C,* or into mainstream classes, as quickly as possible. Review, self-assessment, and culminating student projects end each chapter.

 B. *Teacher Resource Book*

The *Teacher Resource Book* contains extensive and detailed lesson plans to guide instruction. Each lesson plan consists of a materials list; chapter topics; learning strategies; and listening, speaking, reading, writing, and viewing skills. The lesson plans include step-by-step teaching suggestions, numbered **Audioscripts,** and page references to **Reading Fluency Teacher Notes,** the *Activity Book,* and the **Mini-Readers.**

Numerous **Culture Notes** appear throughout the lesson plans, with facts and insights to share with students about cultural attitudes, similarities, and differences. A major purpose of the **Culture Notes** is to promote sensitivity and understanding of the richness of diverse backgrounds. Specific teaching tips are highlighted in reference boxes labeled **Grammar, Literacy, Punctuation Notes, Pronunciation Pointers,** and **Spelling Rules.** An important teacher aid is found in the **Language Transfer and Interference** boxes, where explicit information and examples from various languages are cited. Each chapter culminates with a **Viewing Activity.**

Teachers can use the **Reading Fluency Teacher Notes** to implement fluency practice activities in the classroom. For teacher convenience, the *Teacher Resource Book* also contains answer keys for the *Activity Book* exercises.

In addition, the *Teacher Resource Book* provides photocopiable masters of useful graphic organizers that aid in concept development and learning. The use of graphic organizers is especially important to basic-level language learners because they often cannot grasp content through linguistic input alone. The graphic organizers provide visual scaffolding to aid comprehension and language acquisition. Other photocopiable masters include writing lines, letter- and number-formation practice sheets, word tiles, and a blank calendar.

A page of instructions for a variety of literacy and vocabulary development activities completes the *Teacher Resource Book.*

The sixty-one transparencies available in the *Visions Basic Transparencies*—including all of the photocopiable masters—support the *Student Book* and *Teacher Resource Book* by providing an alternative presentation method and group learning experiences. They can be used to:

a. practice and review materials such as alphabet and numeral writing practice, phonemic practice, high-frequency word activities, and personal dictionary forms;

b. teach capitalization and punctuation rules, sentence building, synonyms, and antonyms; and

c. present graphic organizers such as cluster maps, sense charts, webs.

C. *Activity Book*

The *Activity Book* has two parts: eight pages of activities per chapter and ten **Mini-Readers.** The first part provides follow-up practice exercises, skill reinforcement, and additional teaching opportunities. *Activity Book* pages, indicated by an icon in the *Student Book,* are keyed to specific skills including vocabulary, grammar, word study, reading comprehension, and writing. Many *Activity Book* pages also extend and expand the *Student Book* with instruction in spelling, punctuation, and capitalization; readings in content areas; and supplemental vocabulary development. These expansion activities can be augmented further with group work using the *Visions Basic Transparencies.*

A reading fluency activity for each chapter, **Build Reading Fluency,** is an additional element of the *Activity Book.* For new readers, fluency is an important skill that will aid their reading comprehension. The purpose of fluency practices is to help students progress from reading letter-by-letter and word-by-word to reading smoothly and automatically with accuracy, expression, and comprehension.

The second part of the *Activity Book* consists of ten **Mini-Readers**—eight-page reading "books," one for each *Student Book* Chapter 1–10. These short books allow students to apply their new decoding, word attack, and sight recognition skills to engaging stories related to their new environments at school, at home, and in their community.

D. Chapter Organization

1. Chapter Opener

In Chapters 1–10, each opening page presents photographs depicting aspects of the theme and labeled with key vocabulary. In addition, the list of learning objectives previews the content, skills, and strategies presented and practiced in the chapter. In Chapters A–D, the opener teaches the essential chapter vocabulary visually and provides a context for the chapter.

2. Listen, Speak, Interact

Using vocabulary and visual cues from photographs on the facing page, ***Listen, Speak, Interact*** provides controlled and guided auditory and oral practice of vocabulary and authentic conversations. Exercises move first from simple listening and repeating, to second listening, reading, and repeating, to third partner work using substitutions to create new sentences. In later chapters, group work extends these activities to more creative and open-ended use of language.

As the chapters progress, students practice new language functions, vocabulary, and structures and build on what has been presented and learned in previous chapters. This purposeful recycling facilitates students' language mastery. For additional listening and speaking activities to use with Chapters 1–10, see the *Student CD-ROM*.

3. Build Vocabulary

In *Visions Basic*, vocabulary instruction focuses on understanding new words in context and in relationship to other words in that context. By learning vocabulary in semantic groupings, students retain and expand their working knowledge. Contextualized vocabulary development also addresses a critical area identified by research: providing opportunities to study vocabulary meanings and concepts by relating them to prior knowledge and experience, and recording them in a **Personal Dictionary.** For Chapters A, B, C, and D, the *Student CD-ROM* contains additional vocabulary-building expansion exercises.

4. Grammar Focus

A grammar box introduces a beginning-level structure simply and graphically, accompanied by a brief explanation, a recognition activity, and productive use of the structure in context. The structures taught include simple and continuous tenses, nouns and pronouns, adjectives, *-ing* spelling rules, and *There is/There are.* The *Activity Book* provides two pages of review, reinforcement, and expansion activities for each ***Grammar Focus.*** Additionally, the *Student CD-ROM* provides students with direct practice of grammar taught in each chapter.

5. Word Study

In *Visions Basic,* ***Word Study*** phonics instruction teaches the relationships between sounds (phonemes) and letters (graphemes). It proceeds through initial, medial, and final consonants; long and short vowels; blends; diagraphs; and consonant clusters. Compound words, plural count nouns, the prefix *re-*, and the suffix *-er* are also covered.

In Chapters 1–10 of *Visions Basic,* ***Word Study*** continues examining the basic sound/symbol relationships of the English phonological system that were introduced in the preliminary Chapters A–D. As students develop knowledge of the correspondence between sounds and printed symbols, they also develop skills to deal with prefixes, suffixes, and root words. The primary purpose of ***Word Study*** is to provide students with the skills to analyze vocabulary in greater detail according to state standards and to prepare students for state achievement tests. For additional word study activities to use with Chapters 1–10, see the *Student CD-ROM.*

6. Into the Reading: Use Prior Knowledge

Into the Reading: **Use Prior Knowledge** helps students tap into their experiences as they prepare to engage with a new, authentic reading. Questions in the text help students organize their prior knowledge as a strategic aid to comprehension. Students answer questions to share vocabulary related to personal experiences in daily life, such as foods, feelings, relationship terms, and daily routine activities. They also learn to use graphic organizing techniques for representing their ideas and experiences with word webs, Venn diagrams, and simple charts.

Some chapters also contain **Strategy** boxes that present concise reading strategies to help students approach the reading passage. The strategy is then practiced as the students read. These strategies include **Use Prior Knowledge, Preview Questions and Preview Pictures, Scan for Information, Use a Dictionary,** and **Predict.**

7. Into the Reading: Build Background

Each reading in *Visions Basic* is preceded by an activity to help students gain background about the reading selection. **Build Background** is supported and clarified by a picture or diagram that aids comprehension of critical vocabulary or concepts underlying the reading.

8. Reading and Understanding: Text Structure

Text Structure introduces and analyzes distinguishing features of the text. Genres and literary terms are examined. These selections were chosen from various state standards and tests.

9. Reading and Understanding: Reading

Visions Basic provides a range of adapted and authentic readings that are models of the chapter's text structure, including fiction selections (e.g., poems, vignettes, myths) and nonfiction selections. The readings often provide a new context for applying the vocabulary, grammar, and phonics that students have just learned.

The reading fluency exercise for this section of the chapter is found in the *Activity Book*. Research indicates that repeated, guided oral reading and texts that recycle vocabulary are the most effective methods for developing fluency. Teaching notes for improving reading fluency can be found in the *Teacher Resource Book,* pages 126–135. Students can record their fluency progress on a Reading Fluency Chart found on page 125.

10. Reading and Understanding: Beyond the Reading

Reading comprehension in *Visions Basic* focuses first on literal information questions based on the reading. Later, **Beyond the Reading** asks students to compare, explain, and make inferences; as well as use reading skills such as scanning for, and charting, information; retelling a story; and sequencing. Students retell or summarize the reading and may act it out.

11. From Reading to Writing

Here students practice authentic writing by applying concepts learned throughout the chapter and recycling concepts from previous chapters. Students employ a guided process-writing approach: making a writing plan (often with a graphic organizer), drafting, editing, and publishing their efforts. Developmentally expanding checklists provide assistance in self-editing and peer editing of writing. The *Student CD-ROM* enhances students' writing efforts with spelling and punctuation activities, which can be further practiced on related transparencies.

12. Review, Assess, Mini-Readers and Projects

Students using *Visions Basic* complete each chapter by reviewing new vocabulary, expressions, grammar, and word study topics, and then taking a self-assessment. Remediation is referenced to the page where the concept was taught, so students can return to them and review them.

Students can follow up their reading skills with a story from the **Mini-Readers** in the *Activity Book,* beginning on page 113; **Mini-Readers** are correlated to Chapters 1–10. Students use **Mini-Readers** to practice applying new knowledge in a new reading experience. Each **Mini-Reader** is made from two book-pages that students cut, fold, and construct into eight-page booklets. **Mini-Readers** extend each chapter with a lively, student-centered story, followed by comprehension questions, a word study activity, and a self-correction assessment.

The final two pages of each chapter offer two culminating ***Projects*** that require students to integrate and apply their new skills. Each **Project** utilizes the strengths of a different learning style and offers opportunities to work individually, with partners, or in groups. The projects were designed to prepare students for the type of academic project they will encounter in the mainstream classroom. Checklists support their self-evaluation. Students can also refer to the *Visions Student Handbook.*

Try It Out

Teacher Activity: Scavenger Hunt

Use the *Visions Basic Student Book.* Look for activities where the graphic organizers below are used. Write the page number and type of activity. You have four minutes to complete as many as you can.

Graphic Organizer	Book/Page #/Activity
1. Venn Diagram	
2. Word Web or Concept Wheel	
3. Cluster Map	
4. Timeline	
5. Sunshine Organizer	
6. Other	

Teacher Reflections

Discuss these questions with your colleagues.

1. Which organizers did you see most often in the book?
2. Which ones are found in *Visions Transparencies?* Where else might you find them?
3. Why do graphic organizers work so well with beginning learners?
4. How might you explain how to use the graphic organizers to your class?
5. What other types of organizers have you used? What activities did you use them for?

MODULE V Teaching with *Visions Basic:* Chapter A

Module V provides a step-by-step guide for implementing both the first part of *Visions Basic,* Chapters A–D, and the second part, Chapters 1–10. Chapter A and Chapter 1 will be used as model "walk-throughs," so teachers new to *Visions* can learn how to teach both types of chapters and use all chapter components effectively.

A. Chapter A: At School

(*Basic Student Book,* pages 2–13, and *Teacher Resource Book:* Lesson Plans, pages 1–10)

➤ Go to: *Teacher Resource Book,* page 1, ***Chapter A: At School***

Assemble the books and materials of the *Visions Basic* program listed under Materials on this page. Bookmark relevant pages. Bring in supplementary materials, such as newspapers, magazines, food containers, and advertisements as examples of environmental print.

Introductory Activities (*Teacher Resource Book,* page 2)

Have students find and identify letters on signs, posters, cartons, or other items of environmental print.

> On the board, ***write:*** *t.* ***Say:*** *This is the letter* t. Point to a *t* elsewhere in the classroom. Gesture to your eyes as you say *look.* Show *t* and other letters. Each time you point to a letter ***ask:*** *Is this* t? Gesture around the room. Gesture to your eyes as you ***say:*** *Look for another* t.

Encourage students to walk around and point out the letter. Repeat for one or two other letters. Remember to use very few words and lots of gestures with newcomers. Smile encouragingly and nod your head when they respond correctly. Enthusiastically respond with phrases like *Right! Good job!*

TIP This print-awareness activity is only appropriate with students who have minimal or no school experience. See page 45 in Module IV.

1. Chapter A: At School (*Basic Student Book,* pages 2–3, and *Teacher Resource Book,* page 2)

Begin to teach classroom directions. Teach the word *book.* Hold up the student book.

> ***Say:*** *This is a* book. Open your book as you ***say:*** *Open the book.* When everyone's book is open, ***say:*** *Close the book.*

Practice opening and closing books several times. When your book is closed, point to a student. Indicate you want him or her to tell you to open the book. Prompt if needed. Then point between two other students to practice. Do this several times.

Write the number 2 on the board. As you open your book to page 2, ***say:*** *Open the book to page 2.* Show the class the correct page. Circulate and monitor students. Then repeat the process until everyone can find page 2 easily.

During the lesson, make gestures or give nonverbal cues to guide students as you conduct the class, such as pointing to your ear for *Listen* or moving your hand for *Repeat.* Repeat activities as needed. Use the same language each time.

❶ Listen and point. (*Basic Student Book,* page 2)

❷ Listen and repeat. (*Basic Student Book,* page 2)

See teaching suggestions and Audioscripts 1 and 2 for Exercises 1 and 2 in the *Teacher Resource Book,* pages 2–3.

Model the TPR activity b. *Use visual clues* in the *Teacher Resource Book,* page 2. Make a set of flashcards.

> Make sure you are seated when you ***say:*** *Teachers, stand up.* Stand up and hold up the "teacher" card. Then ***say:*** *Girls, stand up.* Gesture to the girls. Hold up the "girl" card. Holding up the cards, ***say:*** *Teachers, sit down. Boys, stand up.*

When students are familiar with the commands, have students copy their own set of flashcards. Let different students give directions to the class. Monitor that the correct cards are held up.

Option A Point to the illustration of the teacher on page 2.

> ***Say:*** *Teacher.* Point to yourself. ***Say:*** *Teacher.* Point back to the word *teacher* in the book. ***Say:*** *Teacher.*

Make a sweeping gesture with your hand to indicate everyone and have students repeat as a group. Then point to individual students to repeat. Repeat the word if a student hesitates for more than a few seconds.

Repeat the procedure for the other vocabulary words on pages 2–3.

Option B Play the audio as you follow the directions for Audioscript 1 in the *Teacher Resource Book,* page 2.

> Point to the man in the student book. ***Ask:*** *Is this a girl?* (no) Point to a boy. *Is this a boy or a girl?* (boy) Point to a teacher. *Who is this?* (a teacher) Point to the man. *Is this a man or a woman?* (man) Make a sweeping hand gesture. ***Ask:*** *Are you students?* (yes) ***Ask:*** *Who is a girl/a boy?* (Students can raise hands or point to someone.) Make a sweeping hand gesture. ***Ask:*** *Are we at home or at school?* (school)

TIP Demonstrate the stress difference between *woman* and *man* by clapping a hard clap-soft clap for the two syllables in *woman* and a hard clap for the single syllable in *man.*

TIP If you have Spanish-speakers in your class, ask them for the cognates of school (*escuela*) and student (*estudiante*).

Use the *Activity Book* pages 1, 2, and 3. Make a transparency of **Left to Right Directionality** on page 1. Show the class the transparency. Point to the direction line as you read it aloud. Then point to item 1. Give the students a minute to examine it. Point to the pictures in *correct sequence* and say each number.

Point to item 2.

> ***Say:*** *Look at the pictures.* ***Ask:*** *Where is number 1?* Have a volunteer write *1* on the transparency. ***Ask:*** *Where is number 2?* Have another volunteer write *2* on the transparency. Point to the first picture in item 2. ***Ask:*** *Is this number 3?* (no) Continue with the rest of the page.

Enlarge item 1 (the cake), so it is a large strip of paper. Also make several copies of items 2–4 in strips to use later.

> As you cut the strip into four panels, ***say:*** *Cut the pictures apart. Then put them in order.*

Rearrange the panels in correct sequence from left to right. As you put each one down, say its number. Make sure all the students see the sequencing. Then pick up the papers, shuffle them, and give them to a volunteer.

> ***Say:*** *Put them in order.* Do this with several volunteers.

Distribute the strips of items 2–4.

> ***Say:*** *Cut the pictures apart. Then put them in order.* Give the students markers and tape or glue to color and paste them on cardboard. Hang them around the room.

Write: 2. Show the *Activity Book*. As you open the book, point to the number 2 on the board. ***Say:*** *Open the book to page 2.* Read the direction aloud. As you ***say:*** *Which way do they go? Draw the line,* use your finger to model the correct way to go across and down the page.

Then read the directions again and indicate to the students to draw the line with their fingers. Have several students model the activity.

Try to start the movement from the bottom up. ***Ask:*** *Is this the way they go?* (no) Then instruct students to draw the line.

Write: 3. Point to Shape Recognition on page 3. Model looking at and circling the letters before assigning the page as individual work.

2. Letters and Sounds (*Basic Student Book,* pages 4–5, and *Teacher Resource Book,* pages 4–5)

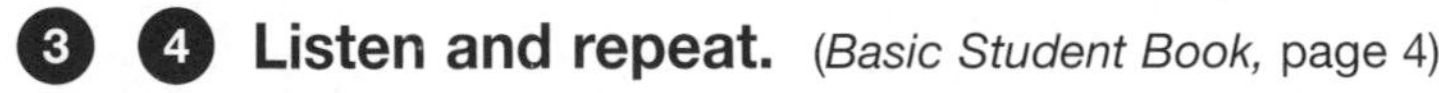

3 4 Listen and repeat. (*Basic Student Book,* page 4)

See suggestions and Audioscripts 3 and 4 for Exercises 3 and 4 in the *Teacher Resource Book,* pages 3–4.

Write: 4. As you open your book, point to the number 4 on the board. ***Say:*** *Open the book to page 4.* Show the class the page. Monitor that everyone is there.

Option A Use *Student Book* pages 4–5 to introduce your students to the letter sounds and common words that begin with the initial letter sounds.

Point out and exaggerate, if needed, how the specific letter sounds are made (such as: lip or tongue position, voiced or voiceless, mouth shape).

Check that students can distinguish the sounds before having them produce the sounds.

> ***Write:*** *m, s, t.* Number them *1, 2, 3.*
>
> Point to 1—m. ***Say:*** (the sound) */m/ is one.* Raise one finger as you ***say:*** *Raise one finger for /m/.*
>
> Point to 2—s. ***Say:*** (the sound) */s/ is two.* Raise two fingers as you ***say:*** *Raise two fingers for /s/.*
>
> Point to 3—t. ***Say:*** (the sound) */t/ is three.* Raise three fingers as you ***say:*** *Raise three fingers for /t/.*

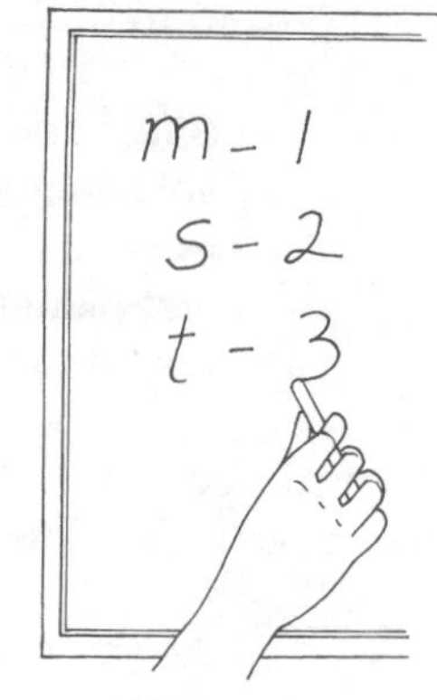

Exaggerate the /t/ as you ***say:*** *teacher.* Have students raise their fingers. Verify their answer by raising your own three fingers. Do this for the other letters. Have volunteers say a sound as the rest of the class raises their fingers.

TIP You can use *school* for this exercise because it is a vocabulary word. Normally, *sch-* is taught as a consonant diagraph cluster. This activity, however, emphasizes 1) the aural discrimination between *m, s,* and *t* and 2) the context and meaning of *school. Sun* and *sat* appear later in this lesson and are good auditory alternatives.

Option B Play the audio as you follow the directions for Audioscript 3 in the *Teacher Resource Book,* page 3. Play it again, and have students listen and repeat. Then point to different letters and ask volunteers to produce the sound and word. Repeat as needed.

Repeat the process with Audioscript 4 in the *Teacher Resource Book,* page 4.

5 Trace. (*Basic Student Book,* page 4)

See teaching suggestions for Exercise 5 in the *Teacher Resource Book,* page 4.

Option A ***Write:*** *M* and *m, S* and *s, T* and *t.* Leave spaces between letters. In a contrasting color, copy the directions arrows from page 4 of the *Student Book.* Point out upper- and lowercase letters. Introduce the terms so students will become familiar with them.

> Using your finger to indicate tracing, ***say:*** *Trace* M. *Trace uppercase* M. *Trace lowercase* m.

Count the number of strokes for each of the letters and give directional words (up, down, across, around) as you model and students practice tracing the letters. If needed, have students trace the letters in the air or on the board before doing the small letters in the *Student Book* on page 4.

Use the *Activity Book,* page 4. Have students complete *Consonants: m, s, t* to practice and reinforce writing the letters and key words.

6 7 Listen and repeat. (*Basic Student Book,* page 5)

Repeat the procedures used in Exercises 3–4 for introducing and practicing letter sounds. Use Audioscripts 6 and 7 in the *Teacher Resource Book,* page 5.

Write: 5. As you open your book, point to the number 5 on the board. ***Say:*** *Open the book to page 5.* Show the class the page. Monitor that everyone is there.

8 Trace. (*Basic Student Book,* page 5)

Repeat the procedures used in Exercise 5 for practicing letter formation of *a, b,* and *g.*

Use Transparencies 1–3 for additional practice.

Complete *Consonants: b, g/Vowel: a,* in the *Activity Book,* page 5, for additional practice and reinforcement.

3. Language and Vocabulary (*Basic Student Book,* pages 6–7, and *Teacher Resource Book,* pages 5–6)

9 Listen and point. (*Basic Student Book,* page 6)

See suggestions and Audioscript 9 for Exercise 9 in the *Teacher Resource Book,* page 5.

Option A ***Write:*** *6.* Open your book. ***Say:*** *Open the book to page 6.* Show the class the page. Monitor that everyone is there. Ask questions about the photos.

> Point to Tran. ***Ask:*** *Is he a boy?* (yes) Point to Ana. ***Ask:*** *Is she a boy or a girl?* (a girl) Point to Lisa. ***Ask:*** *Is she a student or a teacher?* Point to Emilio. ***Ask:*** *Is he a man or a student?*
>
> ***Write:*** *Ana is a _____. (girl, teacher)* ***Say:*** *Ana is a blank.*

Have a volunteer copy *girl,* and read the sentence. After the students can answer easily, let them ask and answer questions of each other.

Option B Play Audioscript 9 in the *Teacher Resource Book,* page 5. Point to the words in Exercise 9 on page 6. Play it again, and have students listen and point.

Role-play the conversation with a student using your own name.

> ***Say:*** *Hi! My name is* (your name). *What's your name?* ***Student:*** *My name is* (student's name). Then use gestures for the student to introduce herself/himself to another student. Have one or two pairs model the conversation. Gesture for the class to stand up. ***Say:*** *Stand up. Repeat the conversation. Say your name. Ask your partner's name.* Circulate and monitor participation. Assist as needed.

Option C Write the lines of the conversation on large strips of paper. Display them in the correct order. Read aloud each line pointing to the words as you read them. Have volunteers come and point to the words as you read them. Say the lines and have students repeat.

Then, cut the strips into words. Distribute the words.

> ***Say:*** *Hi.* Look around to find a student holding *Hi.* Stand the student in the front of the room to hold the word up.

> ***Say:*** *My.* Look around to find a student holding *My.* Stand the student next to the first student.
>
> ***Say:*** *Name.* Look around to find a student holding *name.*

Continue with the rest of the sentence. Soon students will understand you are creating sentences and will come up to take their place in line when you call their word. Have the next group face the first so they can "introduce" themselves.

For additional practice, you can collect the words, shuffle them, and redistribute them. Then ***say:*** *Put the words in order.* Let the students sort themselves into correct order and introduce themselves again.

⑩ Listen and repeat. (*Basic Student Book,* page 6)

See suggestions for Exercise 10 in the *Teacher Resource Book,* pages 5–6. Play Audioscript 10 in the *Teacher Resource Book* on page 6. Have students follow along and then repeat the lines. Repeat as needed.

Option A Model pointing as you ***say:*** *Point to Exercise 10. Point to the direction line over the conversations. Read it with me: Listen and repeat.*

Show that this is the same conversation from Exercise 9 but in a different format.

Point to the *photograph* of Tran in Exercise 9. ***Say:*** *Tran.* Then point to and read from his speech bubble. Then point to the *name* Tran in Exercise 10. ***Say:*** *Tran.* Then point to and read his conversation. Do the same for Ana, Lisa, and Emilio.

⑪ Introduce yourself. (*Basic Student Book,* page 6)

See suggestions for Exercise 11 in the *Teacher Resource Book,* page 6.

> ***Say:*** *Point to Exercise 11.* Point to the direction line over the conversations. Read it aloud.

Write the conversation on the board with the lines for missing names. Then to a student ***say:*** *Hi. My name is (your name). What's your name?* Point to the response and have the volunteer read it filling in his or her name. Then gesture to the student to introduce herself or himself to another student. Continue in a round robin. Then have students copy and complete the sentences in their notebooks.

⑫ Listen and point. (*Basic Student Book,* page 7)

See suggestions and Audioscript 12 for Exercise 12 in the *Teacher Resource Book,* page 6, or follow similar procedures used for Exercises 9–10.

Write: *7.* Open your book. ***Say:*** *Open the book to page 7.* Show the class the page. Monitor that everyone is there.

Before students practice listening and pointing to the words in the conversations, point to the **Words to Know** box. ***Say:*** *Listen and point.* Read the words. Then ***say:*** *Point and say.* Call attention to the letter sounds already studied, for example: */m/ morning, my, Mrs.; /g/ good, Garcia.*

Write: *Good morning. My name is Mrs. Garcia. I'm your teacher.* ***Say:*** *M. Do you see the letter M?* Have a volunteer point out or underline examples in the sentences. Repeat the procedure with other letter sounds previously studied.

Say: *Point to Exercise 12.* Read the directions aloud. Play Audioscript 12 as you point to the words on page 7. Play it again, and have students listen and point.

⓭ Listen and repeat. (*Basic Student Book,* page 7)

See suggestions for Exercise 13 in the *Teacher Resource Book,* page 6.

Say: *Point to Exercise 13.* Read the directions aloud. Play Audioscript 13. Have students follow along and then repeat the lines.

Use names of teachers and staff in the school to practice the courtesy titles. If possible, use photos of the people.

Point to yourself. Use a courtesy title.

> ***Say:*** *My name is* (title and surname). Show a picture of the principal or another teacher. ***Say:*** *This is* (title and surname).

⓮ Listen and repeat. (*Basic Student Book,* page 7)

See suggestions for Exercise 14 in the *Teacher Resource Book,* page 6.

Say: *Point to Exercise 14.* Read the directions aloud. Play Audioscript 14 as you point to the words on page 7.

Option A Ask questions about the photographs. Point to Mrs. Green.

> ***Ask:*** *Is she a woman?* (yes) *Is she a teacher or a student?* (a teacher) Point to Mr. Smith. ***Ask:*** *Is he a boy?* (no) *What is he?* (man) Point to Miss Rana. ***Ask:*** *Is Miss Rana a man or a woman?* (a woman) *Is Ms. Allen a student?* (no) *What is she?* (a teacher)

Play the audio and have students follow along and then repeat the lines. Then say the lines and have students point to the appropriate photos. Point to the photographs. Then point to the line and gesture for volunteers to read the corresponding sentences.

Introduce formal and informal greetings. Model sauntering up and casually greeting a friend with a wave and a "Hi!"

Contrast that with walking carefully and greeting someone with a slight nod and formally saying "Hello."

Point to Ana in the book. ***Say:*** *Hi, Ana.* Point to Mrs. Green in the book. ***Say:*** *Hello, Mrs. Green.* Point to various people in the book and have students greet them appropriately.

4. Letters and Sounds. (*Basic Student Book,* pages 8–9, and *Teacher Resource Book,* pages 7–8)

⓯ Blend the letter sounds. (*Basic Student Book,* page 8)

Bring in pictures or objects to illustrate the meanings of the words in the blending exercise.

> ***Write:*** *8* ***Say:*** *Open the book to page 8.* Show the class the page. Monitor that everyone is there.
>
> Show a baseball bat. ***Say:*** *Bat.* Have students repeat chorally and then individually. Exaggerate each sound by pausing, as you ***say:*** */b/ Pause /a/ Pause /t/.* ***Write:*** *bat.* As you point to the letters individually, ***say:*** */b/ Pause /a/ Pause /t/.* Then sweep your finger under the word as a whole. ***Say:*** *bat.*

Introduce the other words in a similar manner: *man, bag, sat, gas, tag.*

> ***Say:*** *Open the book to page 8. Point to Exercise 15.* Read the directions aloud. ***Say:*** *Blend the letter sounds.* Sweep your finger under the word slowly a few times. Each time, slowly ***say:*** *Blend the letter sounds.* Then sweep your finger fast. Briskly, ***say:*** *bat.*

Play Audioscript 15 on page 7. Have students listen, point, and repeat. Ask volunteers to blend the letter sounds and read the words.

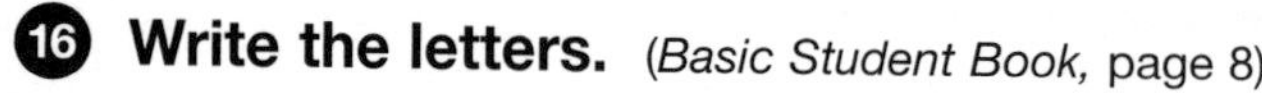

16 Write the letters. (*Basic Student Book,* page 8)

See suggestions for Exercise 16 in the *Teacher Resource Book,* page 7.

Option A Use Transparencies 10 and 11 to model the exercise. Depending on the needs of the students, you may want them to trace the letters in the air or on the board before copying the small letters in Exercise 16. Call attention to the directional arrows on the letters to guide students as they trace and note the height of the different letters. Remind students to say the letter sound as they trace.

> As you write, ***say:*** *A, around and down.* If needed, have students practice writing larger versions of the letters in various media: chalk on the board, crayon on paper, markers.

Have students complete Exercise 16 in the *Basic Student Book.*

Option B Have students work in pairs. To model this activity, have a volunteer turn his or her back to you. ***Say:*** *Write a letter.* "Write" a letter with the eraser end of a pencil on his or her back. ***Ask:*** *What letter?* If the volunteer guesses correctly, hand over the pencil and turn away. Point to your back. ***Say:*** *Write a letter.*
Then ***say:*** *Write letters with your partner.*

17 Write the words. (*Basic Student Book,* page 9)

See suggestions for Exercise 17 in the *Teacher Resource Book,* pages 7–8.

Option A Display the pictures or objects used previously in Exercise 15 to illustrate the meanings of the words on page 9. Write the words on cards. Hold up the cards one at a time and have volunteers point out the picture or object. Then distribute the cards. Point to an object and have the person with the card hold it up.

Tape the flashcards on the board. Draw three lines after each card. Model and have volunteers model copying the letters to form the words.

> ***Write:*** *9.* ***Say:*** *Open the book to page 9. Point to Exercise 17.* Read the directions aloud. As you point to the first picture, ***say:*** *bat.*

Then point to the word and repeat it. Then with your finger, write *bat* and say it again.

Have students complete the exercise.
Have students make sets of flashcards for the words for additional practice. Students should write the English on one side of the card and translate or draw a picture on the other side.

18 What's the missing letter? (*Basic Student Book,* page 9)

See suggestions for teaching Exercise 18 in the *Teacher Resource Book,* page 8. ***Say:*** *Point to Exercise 18.* Read the directions aloud. ***Say:*** *Look at the picture. Say the word. Write the missing letter.*

Option A Use the pictures or objects and word cards from Exercise 15 to review the vocabulary items. Students can practice matching the pictures/objects and flashcards.
Point to the (picture of the) bat.

> ***Ask:*** *Is this a tag or a bat?* (bat) ***Write:*** *b_t.* Model a think aloud. Point to the bat and ***say:*** *This is a bat. I see the letters b and t. Bat. What's the missing letter? A is missing.* Write in the missing letter. Repeat with other items or pictures.

Option B Use Transparencies 9 and 10 to create letter tiles to form the vocabulary words as you say them and show pictures or objects.
Hold up a bag.

> ***Say:*** *This is a bag. What letters are in bag?* (b, a, g) Model finding the correct letters and arranging them in order to create the word. Repeat with other items.

5. Reading and Writing (*Basic Student Book,* pages 10–11, and *Teacher Resource Book,* pages 9–10)

19 Listen and point. (*Basic Student Book,* page 10)

20 Listen and repeat. (*Basic Student Book,* page 10)

See suggestions for Exercises 19 and 20 in the *Teacher Resource Book,* page 8.

> ***Write:*** *10.* ***Say:*** *Open the book to page 10. Point to Exercise 19.* Read aloud the directions. Play Audioscript 19. ***Say:*** *Point to the letters.* Circulate and monitor that students are following along and pointing to the letters.

Say: *Point to Exercise 20.* Read the directions aloud. Play Audioscript 20. Have students repeat or sing along. Repeat several times. Then sing or chant without the audio.

Option A

> ***Say:*** *Point to* p. *Point to* g.

Repeat for several random letters. Then gesture from one student to another that the first should call out a letter. If needed, ***prompt:*** *Point to. . . .* Then indicate the second student should call out a letter to a third. Continue in a round robin.

21 Write the letters. (*Basic Student Book,* page 10)

See suggestions for Exercise 21 in the *Teacher Resource Book,* pages 8–9.

Write the first few letters, upper- and lowercase, on the board. Copy the arrows in a different color. Model copying *A-a* and *B-b* saying the words *down, across, around* as you do each one. Have volunteers do the next letters in pairs.

> ***Say:*** *Point to Exercise 21.* Read aloud the directions. Circulate and offer assistance as needed.

Use the *Activity Book,* page 6. Have students do *Write the Alphabet* to practice writing the letters. As you gesture first across, then down each line, ***say:*** *Write the letters in order.* This reinforces left-right directionality, so monitor that students aren't going down columns. Use Transparencies 1–3 for additional practice with the alphabet.

22 Point and match. (*Basic Student Book,* page 11)

See suggestions for Exercise 22 in the *Teacher Resource Book,* page 8.

Teach your students how to do a matching exercise.

> ***Write:*** *11.* ***Say:*** *Open the book to page 11. Point to Exercise 22.* Read aloud the directions. Model a match exercise with a two-column chart. In column one, write the uppercase letters *B, G, A, M.* In column two, write the lowercase letters *g, a, m, b.* ***Say:*** *Match upper- and lowercase Bs.* Then draw a line between them. ***Say:*** *Match upper- and lowercase Gs.* Draw a line between them. ***Say:*** *Match upper- and lowercase As.* Hand the chalk to a volunteer to complete.

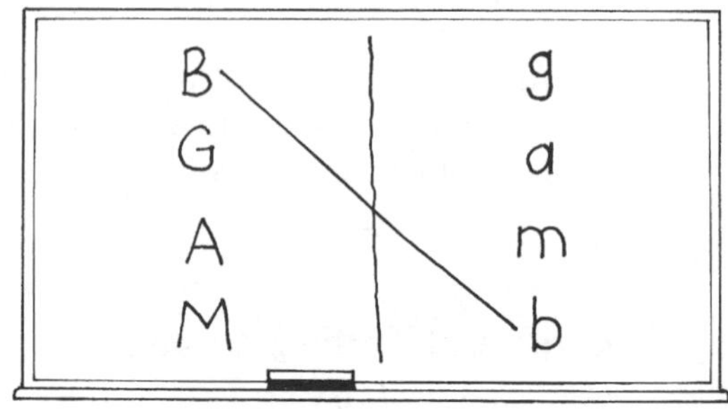

23 Point and match. (*Basic Student Book,* page 11)

See suggestions for Exercise 23 in the *Teacher Resource Book,* page 9.

Option A Write the five words in the first item on the board. Point to the first word.

> ***Ask:*** *What's this word?* (bag) Point to the next word. ***Ask:*** *Is this bag?* (no) *A match?* (no) Point to the next word. ***Ask:*** *What's this word?* (map) Point between *bag* and *map.* ***Ask:*** *A match?* (no) Point to the next word. ***Ask:*** *What's this word?* (bag) Point between *bag* and *bag.* ***Ask:*** *A match?* (yes) *Yes they are a match. Point and match.* Point to both words.

Use the book to repeat the activity with items 2–6.

6. Reading and Writing (*Basic Student Book,* page 12, and *Teacher Resource Book,* page 9)

24 Read and speak. (*Basic Student Book,* page 12)

See suggestions for Exercise 24 in the *Teacher Resource Book,* page 9.

> ***Write:*** *12.* ***Say:*** *Open the book to page 12. Point to Exercise 24.*

Read the directions aloud. Read the conversation aloud once. Act out the two roles by moving from one position to a facing position; using different voices, etc. Then model an exchange with a volunteer. Point to yourself. ***Say:*** *A.* Point to the student. ***Say:*** *B.* Then switch roles. Have students practice in pairs. Ask pairs to present their reading to the class.

25 Write the words. (*Basic Student Book,* page 12)

> ***Say:*** *Point to Exercise 25.*

See suggestions for Exercise 25 in the *Teacher Resource Book,* page 9.

Read the directions aloud. Have students read aloud the words. Model writing the words. ***Say:*** *my.* In the air, write the letters as you say them: M, Y. Then have students practice reading and then writing the words.

Use the *Activity Book,* page 7. Have students do *Write Sentences.*

> ***Write:*** *7.* Hold up the *Activity Book* and open to page 7. ***Say:*** *Open the book to page 7. Point to number 1.* Read item one aloud. Then print the sentences on the board. To a volunteer, ***say:*** *Read number 2.* Write the sentence as the student reads it. Then ***say:*** *Write the sentences.* Circulate and assist as needed.

Use Transparency 4 to give students experience creating sentences.

26 Write the sentences. (*Basic Student Book,* page 12)

See suggestions for Exercise 26 in the *Teacher Resource Book,* page 9.

Point to Exercise 26. Point out the directions. Have students read the question and the answer aloud, saying their own names. Then ***say:*** *Write the sentences in your notebook.*

Use the *Activity Book.* Make a transparency of page 8 to use as a model. Have a volunteer role play the two conversations with you. Then ***say:*** *Match the picture to the words.* Remind students how to draw a match line using your finger. Have a volunteer draw the line on the transparency.

> ***Write:*** *8.* Hold up the *Activity Book* and open to page 8. ***Say:*** *Open the book to page 8. Work with a partner.*

8. Review (*Basic Student Book,* page 13, and *Teacher Resource Book,* page 10)

See suggestions for the ***Review*** in the *Teacher Resource Book,* page 10. If a computer lab is available, assign groups or individuals reinforcement and practice activities on the *Student CD-ROM.*

> ***Say:*** *Open the book to page 13.* Point to the title as you ***say:*** *Review. Point to Review.* Gesture for students to repeat: *Review.* Point as you read the sentence starting, *I can pronounce. . . .* Gesture for students to repeat it.

■ Words

Students can practice reading the words and expressions in pairs. Have them make flashcards with words and expressions. Students should write the English on one side of the card and a picture or a translation on the other side.

■ Expressions

Option A Dictate sentences and have students use their flashcards to make the sentences. Model how to listen to a sentence and find the words from a set of flashcards.

> Slowly ***dictate:*** *I am a student.*
>
> Model looking through a set of flashcards, repeating the sentence to yourself several times. As you find the words you need, say them aloud, and put them down in a row. Then move the words into correct order.
>
> Additional sentences to ***dictate:*** *What's your name? I'm your teacher. I am a girl. I'm a boy.*
>
> ***Say:*** *Now, write* your *name.* Slowly ***dictate:*** *My name is.*

Option B Have students make drawings or use photos of themselves to create posters. Ask students to choose some of the expressions to include on their posters. For example: *Hi. My name is* _____. *What's your name?* Display the posters on a class bulletin board. In small groups, volunteers can present and read aloud their posters.

■ The Alphabet

Option A Do a letter dictation. Model writing one or two letters on the board.

> ***Say:*** *Write the letters.* Slowly ***dictate:*** *lowercase b.* ***Write:*** *b*
>
> Slowly ***dictate:*** *uppercase m.* ***Write:*** *M*

Do one or two additional examples if needed. Then randomly and slowly dictate the upper- and lowercase letters from this chapter: *m, s, t, a, b, g.* If your students are able, add additional letters to the dictation. Be sure to write them as you say them, so you can check them later.

Try It Out

Teacher Activity: What's Your Gesture?

Ask groups of participants to decide on a set of gestures to use as cues in the classroom for various common directions: *listen, repeat, point, read, speak, trace, write.* The goal is to have a visual cue that can be clearly understood and that can be used in a game of Charades.

After groups have decided on their gestures, give a volunteer from each group a direction word to act out for the others to guess.

Teacher Reflections

Think about or discuss these questions.

1. Are there any other gestures that you think will help newcomers adjust to and understand a new school environment?
2. What other directions might you need in the classroom? What are other ways to explain directions?
3. How can you use these gestures and directions to personalize individual activities for new students?

B. Chapter 1: In the School Office

(*Basic Student Book,* pages 52–65, and *Teacher Resource Book* Lesson Plans, pages 39–48)

➤ Go to: *Teacher Resource Book,* page 39, ***Chapter 1: In the School Office***

As with Chapters A–D, the books and materials needed for each chapter are listed under Materials on the first page and should be collected prior to teaching the chapter. Useful supplementary materials to bring in include: student information forms, calendars, office supplies, computers, and office equipment or pictures of the items.

1. Chapter Opener: In the School Office (*Basic Student Book,* pages 52–53, and *Teacher Resource Book,* page 40)

See teaching suggestions and notes in the *Teacher Resource Book,* page 40. Have students keep a record of new vocabulary. Use Transparency #29 or the *Student Handbook,* page 49. They can write or illustrate definitions.

Option A Bring in pictures or actual examples of computers and office equipment or arrange a class visit to the school office. Teach the names of the items as you show or point them out. Hold up or point to the picture of a telephone, keyboard, and mouse.

> ***Say:*** *This is a telephone. This is a keyboard. This is a mouse.* Repeat the names of the items again as you point to them. Then ***say:*** *Point to the mouse. Point to the keyboard. Point to the telephone.* Volunteers point to the items. Point to the keyboard and ***ask:*** *Is this a mouse or a keyboard?* (keyboard) Point to the mouse. ***Ask:*** *Is this a telephone or a mouse?* (a mouse) Point to the keyboard as you ***say:*** *Keyboard. Repeat: keyboard.* (keyboard) Continue teaching the other items using the same procedure.

Write: *52.* As you open your book ***say:*** *Open the book to page 52.* Check that students are on the right page.

Option B Use a TPR activity to reinforce the names and uses of the school and office equipment. This works best with real calendars, staplers, telephones, etc. Array the items around the room.

> ***Say:*** *I need a telephone.* (Students respond by going to the item, and pointing to it and/or saying its name.) *Where's the stapler? May I use the copy machine?*
>
> Use verbal clues and gestures to have students indicate or name the proper school and office equipment. ***Say:*** *Make a phone call.* Raise your hand to your ear as if gripping a telephone. *Print a letter.* Motion from computer to blank piece of paper. *Copy the page.* Point to a page in a book and a blank piece of paper.

When students are familiar with the activity, ask volunteers to act out the uses of the equipment while others name it.

2. Listen, Speak, Interact: In the School Office (*Basic Student Book,* page 53, and *Teacher Resource Book,* page 40)

1 Listen and repeat. (*Basic Student Book,* page 53)

See teaching suggestions and notes for Exercise 1 in the *Teacher Resource Book,* page 40. Play the audio as you follow the directions for Audioscript 1.

Option A Point to the stapler in the *Student Book.*

> ***Ask:*** *Is this a calendar?* (no) Point to the printer. *Is this a printer or a stapler?* (printer) Point to the secretary. *Who is this?* (a secretary) Make a sweeping hand gesture. ***Ask:*** *Is there a calendar here?* (yes) ***Ask:*** *Where is the stapler?* (Students can point to item.)

Option B Point to the photograph of the calendar on page 52.

> ***Say:*** *Calendar.* Point to any example of a calendar in the classroom. ***Say:*** *Calendar.* Point back to the word *calendar* in the book. ***Say:*** *Calendar.* Point out the initial /c/ to remind students of the letter sound.

Make a gesture between students that indicates one student is to point to a calendar and one says the word. Then the speaker points and chooses another student to say the word. Continue in a round robin.

Repeat the procedure for the other vocabulary words on page 52. End the activity by having students choose objects or pictures in random order as others say the words.

Make a transparency of Exercises A and B in the *Activity Book,* page 33. Show the *Activity Book.* Open to page 33 as you ***say:*** *Open the book to page 33. Point to Exercise A.* Read the directions aloud. As you ***say:*** *Put the letters in order. What are the words?* Tell students to write the words.

TIP If you have Spanish-speakers in your class, ask them for the cognates of calendar (*calendario*), secretary (*secretario*), and telephone (*teléfono*).

Option A Point to the direction line of Exercise A in the *Activity Book* as you read it aloud. Then point to item 1. Give the students a minute to examine it. Point to letters in the scrambled version and show how they are reordered to form the names of office equipment.

Point to item 2.

> ***Say:*** *Look at the letters: t-r-e-p-n-i-r. P is the first letter of the word.* ***Ask:*** *What word begins with P?* If needed, students can look on *Student Book,* page 52, to find the correct word. Ask a volunteer to give the next letter and continue spelling out the word. ***Ask:*** *Printer. P. What's the next letter?* (R) ***Write:*** *r.*

Continue with the rest of the letters to form the word. Guide students as needed with the rest of the exercise as they complete the activity in their books.

On the transparency, point out Exercise B and its direction line. Read aloud and have students suggest items in the school office. As volunteers suggest items, demonstrate writing the names of the items in the blank spaces.

❷ Listen and repeat. (*Basic Student Book,* page 53)

❸ Pair work. (*Basic Student Book,* page 53)

See teaching suggestions for Exercises 2–3 in the *Teacher Resource Book,* page 40.

Make a transparency or show an example of a Student Information Form from the *Activity Book,* page 40, or, if possible, the same form your school uses. Have volunteers locate previously learned words: *name, address,* and *phone number.*

> ***Say:*** *This is a form. This is a Student Information Form.*

Play Audioscript 2 in the *Teacher Resource Book,* page 40. Have students point to the words as they listen to the conversation. Then replay the audio and have students repeat the conversation. Point to the Student Information Form as it is mentioned in the conversation. Repeat as needed.

> ***Say:*** *Point to Exercise 3.* Point to the direction line over the conversation. Read it aloud.

Write the conversation on the board with the lines for missing items. To a student ***say:*** *Good morning. May I help you?* Point to the response and have the volunteer read it, filling in one of the school supplies pictured below: pencil, pen, stapler. ***Say:*** *Sure. Here's a (item).* Hand the item to the student. Have the volunteer respond with the last line of the conversation. Then gesture to the student to introduce herself or himself to another student. Continue with others. Then have volunteers play the role of the secretary.

Arrange students in pairs to practice the conversation. Have them switch roles. Finally have students copy and complete the sentences on a piece of paper.

Show the *Activity Book.* Open to page 33 as you ***say:*** *Open the book to page 33. Point to Exercise C.* Read the directions aloud. Point out that this is the same conversation they just practiced. Have them complete the conversation with an item of their choice and practice reading it with a partner.

3. Build Vocabulary: The Calendar (*Basic Student Book,* page 54, and *Teacher Resource Book,* pages 41–42)

4 5 Listen and repeat. (*Basic Student Book,* page 54)

See suggestions for Exercises 4 and 5 in the *Teacher Resource Book,* page 41.

Have students turn to *Student Book,* page 54. Play the audio as you follow the directions for Audioscript 4 in the *Teacher Resource Book,* page 41. Play it again, and have students listen and repeat.

Repeat the process with Audioscript 5 in the *Teacher Resource Book,* page 41.

Option A Show a calendar. Point out the current month and the other months of the year. Have volunteers identify days and months they know. Call attention to the number of days in each week and the number of months in a year. Review counting and introduce the numbers 21–31.

> Point to a day and ***say:*** *Day.* Point to others and ***say:*** *Day.* Point to a column of days, such as Monday. ***Say:*** *Monday.* Repeat with other days of the week. Indicate a circle around all the days on the calendar page and ***say:*** *Month.* Have students repeat the words and days. Repeat with other months as needed. Show all the pages of the calendar and ***say:*** *Year.*
>
> Point to an entire week and ***ask:*** *How many days are in a week?* (seven) Point to each day and guide students to count the days. Show all the months and ***ask:*** *How many months are in a year?* (twelve)

TIP Point out that in English, the days of the week and months of the year must begin with capital letters. Have students compare with their native languages.

Also, in some cultures, the first day of the week is Monday, not Sunday.

Option B Teach the days of the week through song using the tune of "My Darling Clementine." Create a chant for the months of the year with different hand motions such as (touch toes twice) *January, February,* (touch knees twice) *March, April,* (hands on waist one at a time) *May, June,* (hands on shoulders one at a time) *July, August,* (hands on head one at a time) *September, October,* (hands in air) *November, December.*

Have students complete Exercise D in the *Activity Book,* page 33, to practice and reinforce writing the days of the week.

6 Listen and point. (*Basic Student Book,* page 54)

7 Pair work. (*Basic Student Book,* page 54)

See teaching suggestions for Exercises 5–6 in the *Teacher Resource Book,* pages 41–42.

Have students turn to *Student Book,* page 54, Exercise 6. Play the audio as you follow the directions for Audioscript 6 in the *Teacher Resource Book,* page 42. Play it again, and have students listen and point. You may want to make an overhead of the calendar page from the *Student Book,* so everyone can see what you point to clearly.

Say: Point to Friday, January ninth. Have students check with a partner. If needed, point and show the whole class. *Find January tenth. Is it Saturday or Sunday?* (Saturday) *What day of the week is January nineteenth?* (Monday) Point to Sunday, January 4 and ***ask:*** *Is it January eighth or January fourth?* (January fourth) Point to Friday, January 16 and ***ask:*** *What is the date?* (January sixteenth)

Arrange students in pairs to practice Exercise 7 on *Student Book,* page 54. Make copies of Calendar Resource Master (*Teacher Resource Book,* page 163) and have students create a calendar page for the current month. Have them practice using their own calendar pages.

Option A Use Transparency #26 to make a calendar of the current month. Have volunteers point out the current day and say the date. Model the dates and have students repeat. Point out the difference in the counting number (cardinal numbers) and the numbers used in dates (ordinal numbers). Then, say dates and have volunteers point to them on the transparency. Ask students to say the day of the week for various dates. Finally, point to days on the calendar and ask students to give the dates.

4. Grammar Focus: Subject Pronouns and Possessive Adjectives (*Basic Student Book,* page 55, and *Teacher Resource Book,* pages 42–43)

8 Read and find. (*Basic Student Book,* page 55)

See suggestions for Exercise 8 in the *Teacher Resource Book,* page 42.

Make a chart on the board of the subject pronouns and possessive adjectives as you model examples.

Point to yourself and ***say:*** *I am a teacher.* Point to and look at one individual student and ***say:*** *You are a student.* Point to a male student but talk to the others in the class and ***say:*** *He is student.* Point to a female student but talk to the others in the class and ***say:*** *She is a student.* Make a gesture to include everyone including yourself and ***say:*** *We are in the classroom.* Make a gesture to the whole class but not yourself and ***say:*** *You are students.* Point to several students but talk to the rest of the class and ***say:*** *They are in the classroom.* Use the same signals to clarify meanings of the possessive adjectives.

Copy the letter on page 55 on the board. Read the letter aloud. Then do a choral reading. Have volunteers read individual lines of the letter and circle the examples of the subject pronouns. Have others read lines and underline the examples of possessive adjectives in the letter.

Make a transparency of the *Activity Book,* page 34. Read aloud the directions with the students. Clarify and demonstrate the exercises as needed. Have students work in pairs to complete Exercise A. Then have them check their work with another pair.

Assign Exercise B for group work or homework. Additional practice can be assigned from the *Student CD-ROM.*

9 Choose (*Basic Student Book,* page 55)

See suggestions for Exercise 9 in the *Teacher Resource Book,* page 43.

Make a transparency of the *Activity Book,* page 35. For Exercise A, follow the directions for page 34. Have pairs work together to write sentences for Exercise B. Have them share their sentences in small groups.

5. Word Study: Short Vowels (*Basic Student Book,* page 56, and *Teacher Resource Book Basic,* pages 43–44)

10 Listen and repeat. (*Basic Student Book,* page 56)

See suggestions for Exercise 10 in the *Teacher Resource Book,* page 43. Play Audioscript 10 in the *Teacher Resource Book* on page 43. Have students listen and repeat, following the "Short Vowels" box. Repeat as needed.

Option A On the board, ***write:*** *a, e, i, o, u.* Point to the letter *a.*

> *Do you hear a in* cap *or* cup? (cap) *What words have the sound /a/?* (sample answers: address, at, ant, hat) List the words under the letter. Continue with the other short vowels and words.

Guide students to add words with these sounds in the medial position, such as hat, cat, pen, ten, lip, fish, box, hot, cup, bus. Encourage students to refer to their Personal Dictionaries for additional words. Forms and directions for creating Personal Dictionaries can be found in the *Teacher Resource Book,* page 136, on Transparency #29, or on the *Teacher Resource CD-ROM.*

Label the short vowels: 1, 2, 3, 4, 5. Say different words from the list and have students respond with the number of the short vowel.

11 Group work. (*Basic Student Book,* page 56)

See suggestions for Exercise 11 in the *Teacher Resource Book,* page 43.

Option A Have students turn to page 56 in the *Student Book.* ***Write:*** *11.* ***Say:*** *Point to 11.* Read aloud the directions. Ask volunteers to identify the objects in the pictures. Show Transparency #25. Ask volunteers to read the words in the first row. Point to picture 1 in the second row. Have students identify *cat.* Have a volunteer fill in the missing letter. Repeat for pictures 2–5.

Point out the chart. Ask students to find a similar chart in the *Student Book,* page 56.

Help students create their own short-vowel charts. Make copies of the bottom chart on Transparency #25. Have students glue or staple the chart at the top of a sheet of paper to create their own chart headings.

Demonstrate completing the charts with words from the transparency or on the board. Then have students work in small groups to complete the charts.

If some groups are finished before the rest of the class, have them think of other words to add to their charts and make a poster of the chart to hang in the classroom.

Have students do *Short Vowels* in the *Activity Book,* page 36, to practice identifying words with the short vowel sounds. Make a transparency of the page and demonstrate each of the exercises before asking students to complete them.

6. Into the Reading (*Basic Student Book,* page 57, and *Teacher Resource Book,* page 44)

Have students turn to page 57 in the *Student Book.* See suggestions for **Use Prior Knowledge** in the *Teacher Resource Book,* page 44.

■ Strategy: Use Prior Knowledge

See suggestions in the *Teacher Resource Book,* page 44.

Bring in samples of various school forms. Allow time for students to look at the forms and discuss the parts of the forms they recognize.

> ***Say:*** *These are forms. Do you fill out forms?* (yes) *Do you fill out forms at school?* (yes) *At home?* (sometimes) *What are some things you write on forms?* (sample answers: name, date, address) *What else does the school need to know?*

Use gestures and other cues to help students think of other answers. Hold up your hand as if grasping a phone to your ear for *telephone.* Point to a calendar for *date.* Draw a birthday cake for *birth date.* Use the Web on Transparency #28 to fill in the information that students suggest. Then distribute copies of the Web in the *Teacher Resource Book,* page 138. Have students complete their webs with their personal information. Have them compare with another pair of students to see if they have the same or different ideas.

■ Build Background

Hang a sample School Information Form from the *Teacher Resource Book,* page 137, in the center of the board. Sweep your hand over the form.

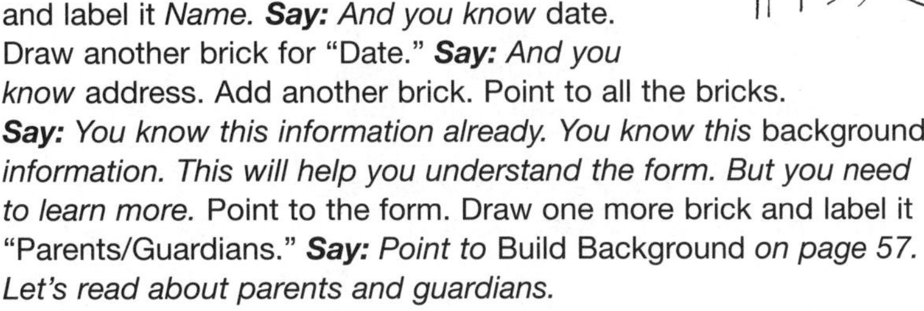

> ***Ask:*** *Do you understand all this?* (no) ***Say:*** *OK, but you know* name. Draw a large brick next to "LAST NAME" on the school information form, and label it *Name.* ***Say:*** *And you know* date. Draw another brick for "Date." ***Say:*** *And you know* address. Add another brick. Point to all the bricks. ***Say:*** *You know this information already. You know this* background *information. This will help you understand the form. But you need to learn more.* Point to the form. Draw one more brick and label it "Parents/Guardians." ***Say:*** *Point to* Build Background *on page 57. Let's read about parents and guardians.*

7. Reading and Understanding (*Basic Student Book,* pages 58–59, and *Teacher Resource Book,* pages 44–45)

See suggestions for teaching **Text Structure** in the *Teacher Resource Book,* page 44.

■ Text Structure: Form

This is the first time your students will encounter the term Text Structure, and it's important for them to understand its meaning. On the board, ***write:*** *Text Structure.* Then do a Teacher Think Aloud.

Say: *I wonder what* Text Structure *means? I see that a* form *is one kind of text structure. I know what a form is; there's one on the bottom of the page. A form is a special way of writing information. So I think text structures must be special ways of writing.*

To clarify text structure further, bring in examples of poems, newspaper articles, song lyrics, etc.—any text structure that is visually distinct. Hold up the poem.

Say: *This text structure is a poem.* Hold up a newspaper article. **Say:** *This text structure is a newspaper article.* Do the same for your other examples.

You can also show examples from the *Student Book* on pages 72 (poem), 100 (vignette), and 114 (newspaper article).

Option A ***Write:*** *58.* ***Say:*** *Open the book to page 58.* Have student volunteers read aloud: Text Structure: Form.

Option B Bring in samples of various forms: job applications, health forms, bank forms, etc. Allow time for students to examine the forms and discuss what they recognize on the forms and what information appears on all or most of them.

Say: *These are forms.* **Ask:** *What do you see on all these forms?* (sample answers: name, date, address, telephone number) *What things are different on some forms?* (sample answers: parent, guardian, age, employer)

Have students work in pairs. Have them highlight the parts of the forms they know and share their forms with a small group.

■ Reading

See suggestions for teaching **Reading** in the *Teacher Resource Book,* page 44.

Option A Hold up the Student Information Form on page 58 for the students to see. Do a Teacher Think Aloud to guide students to pick out words that they already know and to make guesses about other items.

Say: *I know this is a form. I know forms ask about your name. Do you see the word* Name? (yes) *Point to the word* Name.

Students can point to one or more examples on the form. Repeat the procedure for *Address* and *Phone Number.* Have students point out other words they recognize.

Then point to the three examples of *Name* on the form. ***Say:*** *I see* Name *three times. This person has three names: last name, first name, and middle name: Vega, Ana Luisa.*

Ask students their last names. Then their first names. Ask students to raise their hands if they have middle names. Point out that some people don't have middle names. They leave that box blank on forms. Ask volunteers to state their whole names. You can expand the discussion by asking about nicknames.

Read through the form together in a Read Aloud, pointing to items as you read them on the transparency.

Say: *Student Information Form. Is this a form for students?* (yes)

> ***Say:*** *Date, nine, six, oh, four. I know the word* Date. *I use a calendar to find a date. Today's date is* (the date). *Maybe these numbers on the form tell me the month, day, and year. What is the ninth month—September or December?* (September) *Is six for the day or the year?* (day) *Is the year 2003 or 2004?* (2004)

Continue reading aloud the rest of the form, encouraging students to make guesses about words and meanings.

■ Chapter 1 Mini-Reader: First Day at School.

(*Basic Activity Book,* pages 113–116)

Show students the Mini-Reader for Chapter 1 in the *Activity Book* pages 113–116. Demonstrate and have students cut out pages 113–116 and fold the booklets to create their own Mini-Readers.

Preview the Mini-Reader, identifying people and places in the photos and making guesses about the content.

> ***Say:*** *Point to the title of this Mini-Reader. Read it with me: First Day of School.*
>
> *Look at the photo on page 1.* ***Ask:*** *Are they teachers or students?* (students) *Are they at home or at school?* (at school) *Who is asking, "Where is my first class?"* (the girl). Repeat the procedure for the other pages.

Have students practice scanning.

> ***Ask:*** *How do you scan this reading? What seems to be the important information? How can the pictures help you understand what the reading is about?*

Teacher should allow students to read silently, first. Then, do a jigsaw reading with a different student reading each page.

Arrange students in pairs to re-read the Mini-Reader together.

Make a transparency of the questions on the Mini-Reader, page 8. Read aloud and clarify the directions for each exercise. Demonstrate each of the exercises before asking students to complete them.

■ Beyond the Reading

See suggestions for **Beyond the Reading** in the *Teacher Resource Book,* pages 44–45.

Option A ***Write:*** *59.* ***Say:*** *Open the books to page 59. Point to Reading Comprehension.* Make sure all the students are there.

> ***Ask:*** *What is "reading comprehension"? Do you understand what you have read? These questions tell you if you understand the reading.*

Read the directions aloud. Ask volunteers to read each question. Point out key words in each question. Demonstrate looking back at the form in the reading to find the answers to the questions.

> ***Write:*** *1. Is Ana a student?* Underline the words *Ana* and *student.* ***Say:*** *I see* Student *on the form. Point to the word* student. *Do you see the word* Ana *on the form? Point to her name. Is Ana a student?* (yes)

Continue with the other questions using the same procedure. Then have students work in pairs to answer the comprehension questions.

Have students find the Strategy box on page 59. Have a volunteer read aloud the explanation of scanning. Remind students to look for key words as they scan. Read aloud the directions for this section. Point out key words in the questions for *Scan for information.*

> ***Say:*** *Scan the form for Ana's last name. Last name.* ***Ask:*** *Where is* last name *on the form? Point to it. What is Ana's last name?* (Vega)

If needed, continue with the other questions using the same procedure. Then have students work in pairs to answer the comprehension questions. As students work, walk around the room giving assistance as needed.

Hold up the *Activity Book.* ***Say:*** *Open the book to page 37.*

Play the audio for "Social Studies: Holidays" in the *Activity Book,* on page 37. Replay the audio and have students read aloud with it. Practice scanning by having students find and underline new words in the box. Demonstrate how to answer the questions with the sample that is provided. Have students work in pairs to answer the remaining questions, and have them check their work in small groups. Circulate and offer assistance.

To do "Build Reading Fluency" in the *Activity Book,* page 38, see suggestions on "Reading Fluency Teacher Notes" in the *Teacher Resource Book,* page 126.

Option A Look at the word grid in "Build Reading Fluency" in the *Activity Book,* page 38. Write the five words in the first column of the grid on a column on the board. Point to each word and gesture for the class to say it aloud. Repeat once or twice increasingly quickly. Then point to the words out of order, slowly first, and then more rapidly.

Hold up the *Activity Book.* ***Say:*** *Open the book to page 38.* Read the whole grid aloud as students say it with you. Read the words down in columns.

Then follow the directions in the *Activity Book* to complete Part B.

For Part C use a stopwatch to time half the class as partners listen and check off correct words. Then repeat for the other half.

Have students record results on their "Reading Fluency Chart." Make copies for each student from the master in the *Teacher Resource Book,* page 125, or print off from the *Teacher Resource CD-ROM.*

8. From Reading to Writing: Filling Out a Form (*Basic Student Book,* pages 60–61, and *Teacher Resource Book,* pages 45–46)

■ Writing dates

See suggestions for Writing dates in the *Teacher Resource Book,* page 45.

Option A ***Write:*** *60.* ***Say:*** *Open the book to page 60.* Read aloud the information about writing dates. Point out that the *order* of the dates: *month, day, year,* is the same in both the long and short forms. Guide students to notice similarities between the two forms: day, the last 2 digits of the year. To help students associate the proper number for the months, make a list on the board of the months and their corresponding numbers.

> ***Write:*** *October 15, 2004; 10/15/04.* Point to the month in both forms and ***say:*** *October. Ten. October is the tenth month.* Refer to

the numbered list of months on the board. Point to the day in both forms. ***Ask:*** *Are they the same?* (yes) Point to the year in both forms. ***Say:*** *Two thousand four that's two-zero-zero-four; zero-four.* ***Ask:*** *What is the same?* (zero-four is the same)

Option B Dictate dates using just numbers. For example, ***say:*** *6-4-0-4.* Then dictate the long form. ***Say:*** *June fourth two thousand four.*

Dictate slowly. Then dictate the date and have students write both forms. ***Say:*** *February fourteenth two thousand four.* (Students write: 2/14/04, February 14, 2004)

■ Writing phone numbers

See suggestions for Writing phone numbers in the *Teacher Resource Book,* pages 44–46.

Use the procedure described in **Writing dates** above. Point out parts of a telephone number (area code, phone number) and writing conventions (parentheses, hyphen).

Dictate phone numbers for students to practice writing. Be sure to read the numbers in groups. For example, ***say:*** *Area code: seven-one-eight* (pause) *five-two-one* (pause) *zero-three-four-seven.*

■ Writing addresses

See suggestions for Writing addresses in the *Teacher Resource Book,* page 46.

Option A Bring in maps of the local area, state, and country to clarify the meanings of address components: street, city, and state. Also bring in junk mail envelopes, samples of other mail envelopes, or show the mailing labels on magazines. Point out address components: number, street, city, state, zip code.

Option B Have students practice writing their addresses and then reading and responding to questions about the addresses.

Ask: *Where do you live? What street do you live on?* (student's street) *What city do you live in?* (student's city) *What's the zip code?* (student's zip code) *What's your address?* (Students respond with complete address.)

Option C Make flashcards with the sight words for the components of address: *Address, House Number, Street, City, State, Zip Code.* Show the sight words as you ask the questions above and have students respond with the correct information. Then show just the sight words and have students respond with the correct information about their addresses.

Have students practice writing conventions for dates, phone numbers, and addresses in the *Activity Book,* page 39. Make a transparency of the page. Read aloud the directions and demonstrate the exercises before assigning them.

See suggestions for Filling out a form in the *Teacher Resource Book,* page 46.

Option D Make a transparency of the Student Information Form Resource Master in the *Teacher Resource Book,* page 137, or from the *Teacher Resource CD-ROM.* Make individual copies for the students. Use the transparency to demonstrate filling out the form. Ask volunteers to write personal information. If needed, point out where to write the information. Review proper conventions as needed. Help students with street abbreviations as needed. Then, have students fill out their own information form.

Have students find the Editing Checklist at the bottom of the Student Information Form. Demonstrate on the overhead, checking back to each of the items on the checklist for completeness and correctness. Then tell students to check their own work using the Editing Checklist. Go around the room, helping students as needed.

Have students do *Filling Out a Form* in the *Activity Book,* page 40. Point out that this form is slightly different from the one in the *Student Book.* Ask them to compare and contrast them before completing the one in the *Activity Book.*

> ***Say:*** *Turn to page 40 in the Activity Book.* ***Ask:*** *Do you see the word* Name? (no) *What word do you see?* (student) *In this form, what information goes in the* student *box?* (student's name)
>
> Continue through the form pointing out similarities and differences. Point out the title of this form. ***Ask:*** *Is this information more about the student or the parents and guardians?* (parents and guardians)

Have students work in pairs to use the Editing Checklist at the bottom of page 40 after they have completed filling out the form.

9. Review (*Basic Student Book,* page 62, and *Teacher Resource Book,* pages 46–47)

See suggestions for the ***Review*** in the *Teacher Resource Book,* pages 46–47.

■ Vocabulary

> ***Write:*** *62.* ***Say:*** *Open the book to page 62.* Point to the title. ***Say:*** *Review. Vocabulary.* Point to the sentence. ***Say:*** *I can read and spell these words.*

Students can practice reading and spelling the vocabulary words and expressions in pairs, and giving each other "spelling tests." Have them make flashcards with words and expressions. Students should write the English on one side of the card and a picture or a translation on the other side.

■ Grammar

> Point to the title. ***Say:*** *Grammar.* Point as you read the sentence, *I can use this grammar.*

Have students scan the chapter to find sentences using subject pronouns and possessive adjectives. Students can also practice writing simple sentences using them. Model and write some sample sentences on the board as needed. Have students practice reading aloud their sentences in pairs or small groups.

■ Word Study

> ***Say:*** *Point to Word Study. Read aloud with me. I can pronounce these short vowels.*

Students can use Transparency #27 to help write simple sentences using words with short vowels. Model and write some sample sentences on the board as needed. Have students practice reading aloud their sentences in pairs or small groups.

10. Assess (*Basic Student Book,* page 63, *Teacher Resource Book,* page 47, and *Basic Assessment Program,* pages 19–22)

Make a transparency of page 63. Point out the different sections of the assessment page. If needed, demonstrate one item from each section. Point out the notes about Review pages in the right-hand margin. Have students write their answers on a separate piece of paper or use the sample bubble answer sheet in the *Assessment Program,* page xxi.

Write the answers on the board for a student self-check. The answers can be found in the Answer Key in the *Teacher Resource Book,* page 47.

Visions Basic also provides four-page, multiple-choice quizzes for each chapter, Mid-Book and End-of-Book Exams, as well as *ExamView®*, a CD-ROM that allows teachers to create and customize their own evaluation materials.

11. Projects (*Basic Student Book,* pages 64–65, and *Teacher Resource Book Basic,* pages 47–48)

See suggestions for ***Projects*** in the *Teacher Resource Book,* pages 47–48.

Have students turn to the projects on pages 64–65. Read aloud the title and direction lines before beginning. Point out the samples below to clarify the goal of the project. Be sure students are clear on what they are responsible to do and how much time they have for each step. See more detailed suggestions for the ***Projects*** in the *Teacher Resource Book,* pages 47–48.

Project 1: Make a Class Birthday Book

Have students use drawings or photos of themselves for the class birthday book.

Ask students to draw a picture to describe any special traditions related to birthdays in their native countries. Show American birthday traditions.

Project 2: Make a Class Calendar

Use the class calendar daily to review the date and upcoming school events, holidays, and other special events. Have pairs of students prepare different months to create a class calendar for the entire school year. Post it in the classroom.

Calendar decorations are often related to seasonal weather and activities. Encourage students to compare weather and seasons in the United States with those in their native countries.

Encourage students to fill in announced tests and when special projects are due for different classes on their own personal calendar.

Try It Out

Teacher Activity: Make a Shorter List of Short Vowels

Ask groups of participants to create a list of words that contain examples of short vowels that are used in *Student Book* Chapter 1. Allow five minutes for this. Then, ask them to look back over the list and circle words that might be helpful or useful to reinforce short vowel sounds and cross out words that might be difficult. For example: *September* might be a good word. *December* might not, because the first *e* does not have the short sound. Allow 5–10 minutes for consideration of the words on the lists.

Have groups share some of the words they circled and some that they crossed out and explain their decisions.

Teacher Reflections

Think about or discuss these questions about the Teacher Activity with your group.

1. What were some of the reasons that you crossed off words on your original list?
2. Do you think you might use some of the circled words on your list to reinforce the short vowel sounds? Why or why not?
3. When might it be useful to use additional words to reinforce short vowel sounds? Will this type of reinforcement be useful for all students? Which ones might benefit?

Think about or discuss these issues about student learning:

4. Students at this level often have vastly different language skills. Some will know numbers and dates; others will be more fluent. What are ways that you can utilize these differences in levels for the benefits of all students? Point out specific activities and places in this chapter where you might implement your ideas.
5. What do you feel the role of the native language to be at this level of instruction?

MODULE VI Strategies and Techniques

The *Visions* program provides teachers with a broad range of opportunities for assessing individual progress toward language standards and for engaging students in learning activities. This final section of the *Staff Development Handbook:*

1. explains procedures for assessing students and gives suggestions for using checklists and rubrics;
2. provides information for using graphic organizers;
3. suggests tips for forming and using pairs and groups in the classroom; and
4. discusses other English teaching activities for varying lessons and meeting students' needs.

A. Assessment Rubrics

➤ Go to: **Assessment Reference Chart,** *Visions Assessment Program,* page vi.

Rubrics and checklists can be used to effectively monitor student progress. Each rubric and checklist allows the teacher to set and communicate the goals or standards that students need to demonstrate. These items can help students become aware of their own learning and progress.

Peer rubrics and checklists for students are valuable tools for helping learners collaborate in giving and gaining feedback toward meeting standards. In the **Assessment Reference Chart,** the purposes and pages of the various assessment tools are listed.

1. Checklist Implementation

➤ Go to: **Peer Editing Checklist,** *Student Handbook,* page 12, and *Visions Assessment Program (A, B, C),* page 118, or *(Basic),* page 81.

Make a transparency of an anonymous student writing sample and the **Peer Editing Checklist.** Direct students to follow along on the **Peer Editing Checklist** in the *Student Handbook,* page 12. Give them time to read the checklist over. Then have a volunteer read it, asking for and giving clarification of terms as needed. Demonstrate filling in the writer's and editor's names on the **Peer Editing Checklist** as students follow along in the *Student Handbook.*

> ***Read:*** *1. Is there a title?* Point to various parts of the student's writing sample. ***Ask:*** *Is this the title?* (yes) *What is the title?* (sample answer: "My Best Friend")

Model looking for and pointing to examples of the other items on the checklist. Call attention to the editing symbols at the end of the checklist. As volunteers read aloud, ask for and give clarification of terms and symbols.

Ask a volunteer to read aloud a sentence from the writing sample. Point to various words.

> ***Ask:*** *Is this word spelled correctly?* (no) *What symbol should I use?* (sp) *Do I need a capital letter or a lowercase letter here?* (capital letter) *What symbol do I write?* (cap) Continue with questions about other sentences in the writing.

Be sure that students understand the language and terms used on the checklists. Model examples of each point. In the beginning, limit the number of items to be considered in the self- and peer-editing activities. Later, add more items as students become familiar with the checklists and with the self- and peer-editing procedures.

Have students exchange writings with partners. Allow time for students to read their partners' papers. As students complete the checklist, walk around to monitor their work and to answer individual questions.

Have students give the completed checklist and writing back to their partners. Allow time for students to look over the checklist and make corrections as needed to their writing. Students can hand in a revised or final version of their writing with the original writing and the peer checklist.

2. Rubrics

➤ Go to: **Rubric for Oral Presentations,** *Visions Assessment Program (A, B, C),* page 137.

Distribute a copy of the rubric to each student and make a transparency to use with the group. Review the criteria for assessment and the levels of mastery as they prepare a specific oral presentation. Read aloud, asking for and giving clarification of terms as needed. Point out the criteria items in the first column of the rubric and underline key words.

> ***Say:*** *Presentation. How do I talk to the audience? What is eye contact?* (If students do not guess, point to your eye.) *Do I look at them? That's* eye contact. (Gesture to the chart.) ***Ask:*** *What are gestures?* Demonstrate and ***ask:*** *Why do we use gestures?* (to help people understand, to show things, to add importance)

Continue with other items and key words. Ask students to give examples or to demonstrate.

Call attention to the column headings and point values. ***Say:*** *Three points is very good. Two points is OK. One point means "you need to do more."*

Review the rubric again before students make their oral presentations to the class or group.

If possible, videotaping or tape recording student presentations are effective evaluation tools. Recordings can then be used to assess individual students after they make oral presentations. Students can also use the **Speaking Checklist** on page 2 of the *Student Handbook* to self-evaluate their presentation. Use the rubric and notes to discuss students' presentations and to talk about ways to improve their next presentations.

3. Rubrics for Standards Assessment

➤ Go to: the **Standards Assessment Checklists,** *Visions Assessment Program (A, B, C),* pages 138–144.

To assist with increasing demands for accountability, ongoing records of individual progress over four marking periods are readily maintained on extensive **Standards Assessment Checklists** in *Visions Assessment Program*

(A, B, C), pages 138–144. These **Checklists** include 51 standards related to Listening and Speaking, 65 related to Reading, 78 related to Writing, and 25 related to Viewing.

The **Standards Assessment Checklists** are useful tools to assess where students are and what to teach them. They also let parents know where their children stand and how they are progressing through school. In addition, they also help demonstrate to administrators and others in the educational program that students are learning effectively.

1. Make a copy of the rubric and checklist for each student.
2. Use chapter quizzes, unit tests, informal assessment results, and rubrics to determine students' progress toward attainment of the standards.
3. Note that with the rubrics on the **Standards Assessment Checklist** teachers evaluate each student on his or her own level, not in comparison with others in the class.

4. Portfolio Assessments

➤ Go to: **Portfolio Assessment,** *Visions Assessment Program (A, B, C),* page viii.

The **Student Portfolio** is a place for students to keep their best work as they proceed through the *Visions* program. Students begin this process by keeping all the work they produce as they proceed through a unit (in *Books A, B,* and *C*) or a chapter (in *Basic*). These records of their work can be visual, written, recorded, or taped. Then as a part of an ongoing assessment of their learning goals, students reflect on their work and select at least one example of their best efforts to collect in individual portfolios. The **Portfolio: Activity Rating and Reflection Sheet** in the *Assessment Program Book (A, B, C),* page 115, and (*Basic*), page 82, can be used to help focus and structure their reflections.

Student Portfolios can be another vehicle for parents and school administration to evaluate, assess, and validate student work and progress.

B. Using Graphic Organizers

Refer to: *Visions Teacher Resource Book (A, B, C),* **Teacher Resources,** pages 35–64; (*Basic*), pages 136–147; *Transparencies,* and the *Visions Student Handbook,* pages 8–9 and 15–19.

Graphic organizers guide students in connecting, expanding, and organizing their thoughts and ideas. Students with developing language skills find graphic organizers useful in understanding and processing new language and concepts. The graphics provide a scaffold with drawings, words, expressions, or sentences depending on the students' language skills. Students can then express their ideas in a logical, organized manner by using what they have visually included on their charts or organizers. The layout and format of the charts aid students in communicating their ideas.

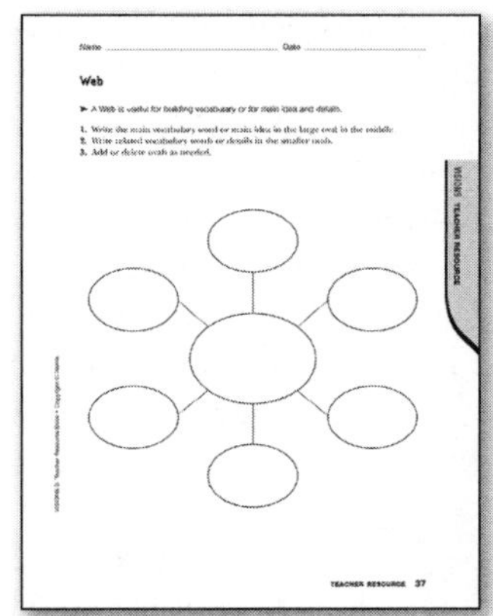

Remember that various organizers arrange information differently, so it's important to model the language and expressions for communicating the relationships and logical organization for each of the organizers.

See the *Teacher Edition (A, B, C),* pages 35–64, for specific organizers and activities.

➤ Go to: **Word Squares,** *Visions Teacher Resource Book (A, B, C),* page 41. Use Transparency #7 *(Visions A, B, C).*

One example of a graphic organizer that helps support vocabulary development is **Word Squares.** First, students jot down a new word in the first box. Next they write the meaning in the second box; the meaning can come from context or from the dictionary. The following two boxes allow for multi-level adaptations. For example, beginning students can draw a picture or a symbol for the word in the third box and write a sentence using the word in the fourth box. More advanced students may write synonyms and antonyms in the third box and add a question in the fourth.

(1) Word	(3) Symbol/Picture or Synonym/Antonym
(2) Meaning	(4) Sentence and/or Question

Word Squares can also be kept on index cards that are divided into four parts.

For an example of **Word Squares,** see *Visions Book A,* page 119.

C. Pair and Group Work

Pair and group work allow students extended opportunities to practice language skills you may introduce in whole class activities. They reduce pressure and fear of making errors in front of a large group. Pair and group work also allow students to share their own ideas and to learn from each other. Below are some suggestions and ideas on forming groups and implementing group tasks.

Set up partners and groups for one or two weeks and then rotate and change groupings. For pair work, have students work with a person sitting next to or behind them. To make small groups, have rows of students arrange their chairs in a small circle. Another grouping technique is to have students count off by fours or fives, depending on class size and the number of groups.

Make sure students understand the activity. Model or demonstrate exactly what you expect students to do or accomplish in their groupings or pairs. Use a volunteer pair to model the task. In some activities, specific roles may be assigned to each member of the group, for example: leader/facilitator (asks questions and leads the activity), recorder (writes or records words and information), reporter (reports information to the class), and timekeeper (watches the clock and makes sure work is on task). Be sure each person is clear about his or her responsibilities.

Be sure students know the time allowed for the specific activity. Set up a clear "zero noise level" signal for ending the pair or group work.

> ***Write:*** *Begin: 10:15. End: 10:25.* ***Say:*** *Now it is ten fifteen. At ten twenty-five, we will stop. You have ten minutes to work.*

Notify each group's timekeeper when ten minutes, five minutes, and one or two minutes remain. If students finish before the end time, check their work and suggest they add more details or information, if appropriate. Ask them to create a visual or write their ideas on the board to present to the other groups.

As pairs or groups work, circulate, listen, and monitor. Answer questions, provide support, and make corrections privately as needed, but try to let the groups practice and work collaboratively on the activities rather than being directed by the teacher.

For example, point to a specific item that is not clear on a list or chart.

> ***Ask:*** *What does this mean?* (Student may explain, draw a picture, act something out, look up a word in a dictionary or other resource.) *Can you explain this more? Look at this again. Is this right?* (no) *What should it be?* (Student suggests alternative.) *What else can you add?* (Students brainstorm other items as guided.)

After pair and small group activities, invite pairs and groups to report back to the class what their groups discussed or prepared. Then, guide the group to summarize the results of the activity.

Make a large organizer, or tally chart, on the board.

> ***Ask:*** (Student), *what is on your list/chart/paper?* (Student shows his/her product and identifies items.) Write key words and phrases on the chart. ***Ask:*** *How many groups had this?* Ask other groups for additional points or phrases to include on the board and check on agreement of the ideas. ***Ask:*** *Do you agree or disagree?* (agree) When all ideas are on the board, ***ask:*** *Which idea does everyone think is the most important?* (Students give their choice of main points.)

D. Other Techniques

■ Think Aloud

A **Think Aloud** lets the teacher model the thought processes that a good reader or language learner uses to understand a reading selection, a visual cue, or spoken language. The teacher guides students through a difficult selection by identifying what is unclear, what is known or what clues there are, and what predictions or hypotheses can be made.

Students are exposed to a model of the strategies that can be used to help comprehension. They see that it is all right to stop and use problem-solving skills in their own reading.

Students can benefit from a **Think Aloud** model for making predictions, visualizing or describing a picture as you read, making an analogy to link prior knowledge with new information, identifying main idea and supporting details, making comparisons, contrasting, interpreting literary devices, and guessing meaning of new words from context.

For examples of **Think Aloud,** see Module III, page 24 or *Visions Teacher Edition, Book B,* page 2, side column, **Use Prior Knowledge.**

■ Reading

Partner Read Aloud Students work in pairs. Arrange seats so students are facing each other. As one student reads aloud, the partner listens and follows along in the reading selection. The reader and listener can ask each other for help or clarification as needed.

Reciprocal Reading This activity is more complex than simply reading together. Students need to focus on what they are reading so they can ask questions and help others to summarize and make predictions about a reading passage.

This activity can be done in pairs or small groups. One student is the "teacher/leader" whose job it is to read a short selection and then ask the partner questions about the reading. The roles switch for the next paragraph or selection and the other student becomes the "teacher."

By asking questions about a reading passage, the "teacher/leader" becomes actively involved with the content and responsible for his or her own learning. This helps the student's understanding and recall of the passage. The listener benefits from focusing on listening and reading and then answering the "teacher/leader's" questions about the passage.

Before using this activity, model it with a student. Have students practice scaffolding their questions. Have beginners focus on information questions (*who, what, where, when*) or summarizing questions (*What happened?*). More advanced students can add thinking questions (*How does that ____? Why does it ____?*), clarification questions (*What does ____ mean?*), prediction questions (*What do you think will happen next?*), and summary questions (*What is this paragraph about?*) to their repertoire. Write level-appropriate models on the board for reference.

Model questions of each type for students and have them identify the question types.

Ask: *Who was Anne Frank?* (information) *How did she feel in the apartment?* (thinking) *What did she write?* (information) *What does "symbol" mean?* (clarification) *Why was it dangerous for her family?* (thinking) *Where did she live? When did she live there?* (information) *What will Anne do about this problem?* (prediction) *Tell me what happened.* (summarizing)

See the *Staff Development Video* for an example of a **Reciprocal Reading.**

Popcorn Reading In this group reading activity, all students take turns reading aloud as the others follow along. One student begins reading. The reader continues and then calls out "popcorn" and the name of another student. This new person begins to read and "pops" to another person in the group. Students need to be sure to follow along so they know where to begin when the reading is "popped" to them.

➤ Go to: *Visions B,* page 96. Model this with a few students at the beginning.

> ***Say:*** *I'm going to start to read page 96. Follow along in your books. When I say* Pop, *I will say the name of someone in the group. That person will then read.*
>
> ***Read:*** *August 11, 1609. Today, we came to land at last! It seems there are no bones in my legs.* ***Say:*** *Pop* (a student).
>
> (that student) ***reads:*** *I hugged my friend Jessie. We held each other up.* (that student) ***says:*** *Pop,* (next student).
>
> (next student) ***reads:*** *Still, the land seemed. . . .*

Break-in Reading is a variation of **Popcorn Reading,** allowing for extra support and helping students build up oral reading fluency. One person begins reading aloud as the others follow silently. When someone in the group wants to read aloud, he or she "breaks in" and reads along with the first person. The first person stops reading at the end of the sentence.

At that time, the second person continues reading aloud until another member of the group "breaks in."

Jigsaw Reading In this reading technique, students work collaboratively to understand a long reading selection. Each student reads and studies one designated section of the reading selection or "jigsaw puzzle." Students are then arranged in groups with at least one "expert" on each part of the reading, where they share with the others their part of the reading. After each student in the group has shared, everyone has learned about the entire reading selection. Each member is responsible and has an integral part of the learning process.

a. Divide the class into "home groups."
b. Give each student in the groups an "expert number": 1, 2, 3, 4. . . .
c. Rearrange the class into "expert groups" so all the "ones" form one expert group, all the "twos" form another, all the "threes," etc.
d. Assign each expert group different parts of the reading selection. The parts can range from a paragraph to an entire page. Tell the expert groups to read their assigned part together and make sure they all understand it. (The expert groups can use a technique such as **Reciprocal Reading** to help them master and summarize their assigned portions.) As groups work together, monitor progress and assist as necessary.
e. Return students to their "home groups." Students in the home group share the content and what they learned about their part of the long reading selection in their expert groups.
f. As a whole class, review and summarize the entire reading passage.

See Module V, page 71 for an example of a **Jigsaw Reading.**

5. Shared Writing

A **Shared Writing** (also called **Language Experience Activities** or **Interactive Writing**) uses students' words and expressions as a basis for reading, writing, and language learning activities. After reading a story or participating in an activity, students dictate their own version of the event. The teacher records the students' words and structures. Then students read their story. Students can correct or edit as the teacher discusses and explains problem spots. Later, students copy the corrected text for further reading practice. **Shared Writing** can be done with individual students or in groups or with the whole class.

➤ Go to: *Visions B*, page 39, **From Reading to Writing.** Model the activity with a student. Use a graphic organizer, such as a **Sunshine Chart,** to organize the information.

a. ***Ask:*** *Do you know someone who faced danger?* (Yes) *Who?* (my father) *When? Where?* As the student responds, list words and phrases on the board.
b. ***Say:*** *Let's write the story together.* ***Ask:*** *Who is the story about?* (my father) *What happened?* (My father got lost in the forest.) Use guiding questions and/or gestures to help the student state the story as completely as possible.
c. Write the student's story word for word without changing grammar or adding words.
d. When the student is finished, read the story aloud together as you point to each word. Then have the student read the story aloud. ***Ask:*** *Do you want to change anything?* If so, discuss and make the changes.

e. Have the student copy the story and practice reading it to others.
f. Do other follow-up activities as needed related to vocabulary, phonics and decoding skills, grammar, or comprehension.

6. Think-Quickwrite-Pair-Share

The **Think-Quickwrite-Pair-Share** technique prepares students to write about a topic. It gives time for thinking, jotting down ideas, sharing ideas with a partner, and sharing with a small group. During sharing, students begin to explain their ideas and add details. The sharing helps students develop their ideas for a more formal writing task.

➤ Go to: *Visions B,* page 53, **From Reading to Writing.** Make a copy of the chart from page 53 on the board and give students individual copies. Model the **Think** and **Quickwrite** steps using the chart on the board.

a. ***Say:*** *Living in the city is a challenge for me.* Write your challenge on the chart. ***Say:*** *But I have a map of the city. I can learn the streets. I can ask directions, so I don't get lost.* Write these steps on the chart. ***Say:*** *When I learn more about the city, I will like living in the city.*
b. Give students five minutes to think and write their ideas on the chart.
c. Arrange students in pairs to share the information on their charts.
d. Finally, ask two pairs of students to form a small group to retell their narrative. Have them include other details to their chart as they retell their stories.

Try It Out

Teacher Activity: How Do You Like Your Popcorn?

Ask groups of participants to choose a reading selection from any *Visions Student Book.* Tell them to use **Popcorn Reading** (or **Break-In Reading**) for all or part of the text. Set a ten-minute time limit. After groups have completed their reading, have them discuss the questions below.

Teacher Reflections

Discuss these questions with your group.

1. What did you like about this technique for reading with a group? What didn't you like?
2. Do you think students would like this technique? Why or why not?
3. Would you ever set a minimum or maximum number of words for students to read before they say "pop"? Why?

Bibliography

Allen, J. *Words, Words, Words: Teaching Vocabulary in Grades 4–12.* Portsmouth, NH: Heinemann, 1999.

Celce-Murcia, M. "Grammar Pedagogy in Second and Foreign Language Teaching." *TESOL Quarterly,* 25(1991): 459–480.

Cummins, J. "Knowledge, power, and identity in teaching English as a second language." *Educating Second Language Children: The Whole Child, The Whole Curriculum, The Whole Community.* Ed. F. Genesee. New York: Cambridge UP, 1994.

Decarrico, J. "Vocabulary Learning and Teaching." *Teaching English as a Second or Foreign Language,* 3rd ed. Ed. M. Celce-Murcia. Boston, MA: Heinle, 2001.

English-Language Arts Content Standards for California Public Schools Kindergarten Through Grade Twelve, Sacramento, CA: California DOE, 2001.

Fowler, B. "Bloom's Taxonomy and Critical Thinking (Questions)." *Critical Thinking Across the Curriculum Home Page.* Longview Community College, 1996. <http://www.kcmetro.cc.mo.us/longview/ctac/blooms.htm>

Gardner, H. *Intelligence Reframed: Multiple Intelligences for the 21st Century.* New York: Basic, 2000.

Gibbons, P. *Learning to Learn in a Second Language.* Portsmouth, NH: Heinemann, 1993.

Hedge, T. *Teaching and Learning in the Language Classroom.* New York: Oxford UP, 2001.

Kinsella, K. "Academic Vocabulary Development to Support Reading and Learning from Texts." Handout presented at a workshop at the Standards-Based Evaluation and Accountability Institute. Santa Barbara, CA., December 4, 2001.

Lindsay, P. *Teaching English Worldwide.* Burlingame, CA: Alta Book Center Publishers, Longman, 2000.

McCloskey, M. L. & Stack, L. *CNN Video to Accompany Visions.* Boston: Heinle, 2003a.

—*Visions: Language, Literature, Content.* Boston, MA: Heinle, 2003b.

National Reading Panel. *Teaching Children to Read: An Evidence-based Assessment of the Scientific Research Literature on Reading and Its Implications for Reading Instruction* (National Institute of Health Publ. No. 00-4769). Washington, DC: 2002 National Institute of Child Health and Human Development.

Schmitt, N. "Vocabulary Learning Strategies." *Vocabulary: Description, Acquisition, and Pedagogy.* Eds. Schmitt & McCarthy. Cambridge: Cambridge UP, 1997.

Strategic Teaching and Learning. Sacramento, CA: California DOE, 2000.

Additional References

Agor, B. *Integrating the ESL Standards into Practice, Grades 9–12.* Alexandria, VA: ASCD, 2000.

Anderson, N. *Exploring Second Language Reading: Issues and Strategies.* Boston: Heinle, 1999.

Anderson, N. J. The Role of Metacognition in Second Language Teaching and Learning. *Eric Digest* EDO-FL-01-10, 2002. Access at: <http://www.cal.org/ericcll/digest/0110anderson.html>

Asher, J. J. *Learning another language through actions: the complete teacher's guidebook* 2nd Edition. Las Gatos, CA: Sky Oaks, 1983

Atwell, N. *In the Middle.* Portsmouth, NH: Heinemann, 1987.

Au, K. H. *Literacy Instruction in Multicultural Settings.* Fort Worth, TX: Harcourt, 1993.

Auman, M. *Step Up to Writing.* Longmont, CO: Sopris West, 1999.

Bailey, K. M. & Savage, L., eds. *New Ways in Teaching Speaking.* Alexandria, VA: TESOL, 1994.

Boswood, T., ed. *New ways of using computers in language teaching.* Alexandria, VA: TESOL, 1999.

Brown, H. D. *Principles of Language Learning and Teaching.* 3rd Edition. Prentice, 1994.

—*Teaching by Principles,* 2nd ed. Englewood Cliffs, NJ: Prentice, 2001.

Buss, K. & Karnowski, L. *Reading and Writing Nonfiction Genres.* Newark, DE: IRA, 2002.

Calkins, L. *The Art of Teaching Writing.* Portsmouth, NH: Heinemann, 1986.
Campbell, K. U., *et al.* "Effects of a Reading Fluency Intervention for Middle Schoolers With Specific Learning Disabilities." *Learning Disabilities Research and Practice,* 15 (4) (2000): 179–189.
Canale, M. & Swain, M. *Communicative Approaches to Second Language Teaching and Testing.* Toronto: Ministry of Ed. 1980.
Chamot, A. U., *et al.* "Methods for Teaching Learning Strategies in the Foreign Language Classroom," *Language Learning Strategies Around the World: Cross-Cultural Perspectives.* Ed. R. Oxford. Manoa, HI: U. Hawaii Press, 1996.
Claire, E. *ESL Teacher's Activities Kit.* Englewood-Cliffs, NJ: Prentice, 1999.
Cohen, A. D. *Strategies in Learning and Using a Second Language.* New York: Longman, 1998.
Connor, U. & Kaplan, R., eds. *Writing Across Languages: Analysis of L2 Text.* Reading, MA: Addison-Wesley, 1987.
Cummins, J. "e-Lective Language Learning: Design of a Computer Assisted Text-Based Esl/Efl Learning System," *TESOL Journal,* Spring, 1998.
Cummins, J. & Sayers, D. *Brave New Schools: Challenging Cultural Illiteracy Through Global Learning Networks.* New York: St. Martin's, 1997.
De Jong, E. & Harper, C. Preparing Mainstream Teachers for English Language Learners: a Matter of "Just Good Teaching"? (Unpublished manuscript.)
Egbert, J. & Hanson-Smith, E., eds. *CALL Environments: Research, Practice, and Critical Issues.* Alexandria, VA: TESOL, 1999.
Elley, W. B. "Acquiring Literacy in a Second Language: The Effect of Book-Based Programs." *Language Learning,* 41 (1991): 375–411.
Ellis, R. "The Place of Grammar Instruction in the Second/Foreign Language Curriculum." *New Perspectives on Grammar Teaching in Second Language Classrooms.* E. Hinkel & S. Fotos, eds. Mahwah, NJ: Lawrence Erlbaum, 2002.
Enright, D. S. & McCloskey, M. L. *Integrating English: Developing English Language and Literacy in the Multilingual Classroom.* Reading, MA: Addison-Wesley, 1988.
Fillmore, L. W. & Snow, C. E. *What Every Teacher Should Know About Language.* Washington, DC: Center for Applied Linguistics, 2000. Access at: <www.cal.org/ericcll/teachers/teachers.pdf>
Fountas, I. C. & Pinnel, G. S. *Guided Reading.* Portsmouth, NH: Heinemann, 1996.
Freeman, D. & Freeman, Y. *Teaching Reading in Multilingual Classrooms.* Portsmouth, NH: Heinemann, 2000.
Genesee, F. & Hamayan, E. V. "Classroom-based Assessment," *Educating Second Language Children: The Whole Child, The Whole Curriculum, The Whole Community.* Ed. F. Genesee. New York: Cambridge UP, 1994.
Gibbons, P. *Scaffolding Language, Scaffolding Learning: Teaching Second Language Learners in the Mainstream Classroom.* Portsmouth, NH: Heinemann, 2002.
Graves, D. *Writing: Teachers and Children at Work.* Portsmouth, NH: Heinemann, 1983.
Healey, D. & Klinghammer, S. J. "Constructing Meaning with Computers," *TESOL Journal,* 11 (2002): 3.
Hunt, A. & Beglar, D. "Current Research and Practice in Teaching Vocabulary," *The Language Teacher Online.* 2003. Access at <http://www.jalt-publications.org/>
Hymes, D. H., ed. *Reinventing Anthropology.* New York: Pantheon, 1972.
Irujo, S., ed. *Integrating the ESL Standards into Classroom Practice, Grades 6–8.* Alexandria, VA: TESOL, 2002.
Johns, A. "Teaching Classroom and Authentic Genres: Initiating Students into Academic Cultures and Discourses." *Academic Writing in a Second Language.* Eds. D. Belcher & G. Braine. Norwood, NJ: Ablex, 1995.
Kagan, S. *Cooperative Learning: Resources for Teachers.* Rev. ed. Laguna Miguel, CA: Kagan, 1997.
Kamil, M. I. & Bernhardt, E. B. "Reading Instruction for English-Language Learners." *Teaching Reading in the 21st Century.* Eds. M. G. Graves, *et al.* Needham Heights, MA: Pearson, 2001.
Kinsella, K. "Active Learner Strategies for School Success." Presentation at the TESOL Annual Convention, 1998.
Kutz, E., Groden, S., & Zamel, V. *The Discovery of Competence: Teaching and Learning With Diverse Student Writers.* Portsmouth, NH: Boynton/Cook, 1993.
Law, B. & Eckes, M. *Assessment and ESL: A Handbook for K–12 Teachers.* Winnipeg, Manitoba, Canada: Peguis, 1995.
Lazaraton, A. "Teaching Oral Skills." *Teaching English as a Second or Foreign Language,* 3rd ed. Ed. M. Celce-Murcia. Boston, MA: Heinle, 2001.

Lee, K. "English Teachers' Barriers to the Use of Computer-assisted Language Learning." *The Internet TESL Journal, VI* (2000): 12. <http://iteslj.org/>

Leki, I. "Cross-talk: ESL Issues and Contrastive Rhetoric." *Writing in Multicultural Settings.* Eds. C. Severino, J. Guerra, and J. Butler. New York: MLA, 1997.

Li, D. and Nes, S. "Using Paired Reading to Help ESL Students Become Fluent and Accurate Readers." *Reading Improvement* 38 (2001): 50–61.

Lightbown, P. M. & Spada, N. *How Languages Are Learned* (2nd ed.). New York: Oxford UP, 1999.

Lipsey, M. W. & Wilson, D. B. "The Efficacy of Psychological, Educational and Behavioral Treatment: Confirmation From Meta-Analysis." *American Psychologist, 48* (12) (1993): 1181–1209.

Liu, M., Moore, Z., Graham, L., & Lee, S. "A Look at the Research on Computer-Based Technology Use in Second Language Learning: A Review of the Literature from 1990–2000." *Journal of Research on Technology in Education, 34* (2003):3.

Marzano, R. J., *et al. Classroom Instruction That Works: Research-Based Strategies for Increasing Student Achievement.* Alexandria, VA: ASCD, 2001.

McCloskey, M. L. (2000). The Surrender Speech of Chief Joseph. [WebText] Available: <http://www.gsu.edu/%7Eeslmlm/chiefjoseph.html>

McCloskey, M. L. & Stack, L. *Visions: Language, Literature, Content.* Boston, MA: Heinle, 2003a.

McCloskey, M. L. & Stack, L. *CNN Video to Accompany Visions.* Boston: Heinle, 2003b.

McCloskey, M. L. & Thrush, E. (2000). WebTexts: Using Technology to Scaffold English Language Learning. Available: <http://www.mindspring.com/~mlmcc/WebTexts_files/frame.htm>

Morley, J. "Aural Comprehension Instruction: Principles and Practice." *Teaching English as a Second or Foreign Language,* 3rd ed. Ed. M. Celce-Murcia. Boston, MA: Heinle, 2001.

Nuthall, G. "The Way Students Learn. Acquiring Knowledge From an Integrated Science and Social Studies Unit," *Elementary School Journal,* 99(4) (1999): 303–341.

O'Malley, M. & Valdez-Pierce, L. *Authentic Assessment for English Language Learners: Practical Approaches for Teachers.* Reading, MA: Addison-Wesley, 1996.

Oxford, R. L. "Language Learning Styles and Strategies." *Teaching English as a Second or Foreign Language,* 3rd ed. Ed. M. Celce-Murcia. Boston, MA: Heinle, 2001.

Oxford, R. L. & B. L. Leaver. "A Synthesis of Strategy Instruction for Language Learners," in *Language Learning Strategies Around the World: Cross-Cultural Perspectives,* R. Oxford, (Ed.) Manoa, HI: U. Hawaii Press, 1996.

Panman, S. & Panman, R. *Writing Guides.* New Paltz, New York: Active Learning, 2000.

Pennington, M. *The Power of CALL.* Houston, TX: Athelstan, 1996.

Pererson, P. W. "Skills and Strategies for Proficient Listening." *Teaching English as a Second or Foreign Language,* 3rd ed. Ed. M. Celce-Murcia. Boston, MA: Heinle, 2001.

Pressley, M., *et al. Cognitive strategy instruction that really improves children's academic performance.* Cambridge, MA: Brookline, 1995.

Raimes, A. *Keys for Writers: A Brief Handbook.* Boston/New York: Houghton, 1999.

Reid, J. *Teaching ESL Writing.* Upper Saddle River, NJ: Prentice, 1995.

Roblyer, M., Edwards, J., and Havriluk, M. *Integrating Educational Technology into Teaching.* Upper Saddle River, NJ: Prentice, 1997.

Rose, D. H. & Meyer, A. *Teaching Every Student in the Digital Age.* Alexandria, VA: ASCD: 2002.

Schleppegrell, M. J. & Colombi, M. C. (Eds.) *Developing Advanced Literacy in First and Second Languages: Meaning with Power.* Mahwah, NJ: Lawrence Erlbaum, 2002.

Scott, W. A. & Ytreberg, L. H. *Teaching English to Children.* New York: Longman, 1990.

Silva, T. "Toward an Understanding of the Distinct Nature of L2 Writing: the ESL Research and Its Implications," *TESOL Quarterly 27*(1993): 657–677.

Slavin, R. E. *Cooperative Learning: Theory, Research, and Practice, 2nd Ed.* Englewood Cliffs, NJ: Prentice, 1995.

Snow, C. E., *et al* (Eds). *Preventing Reading Failure in Young Children.* Washington, DC: National Academy, 1998.

TESOL. *ESL Standards for Pre-K–12 Students.* Alexandria, VA: TESOL, 1997.

TESOL. Assessment and Accountability of English for Speakers of Other Languages (ESOL) Students. TESOL Position Paper. Alexandria, VA: TESOL, 2000. Access at <http://www.tesol.org/assoc/statements/2000-assessment.html>

Trochim, W. M. *The Research Methods Knowledge Base*, 2nd Ed. (version current as of 2000). Access at <http://trochim.human.cornell.edu/kb/rel&val.htm>

Warschauer, M. *E-Mail for English Teaching*. Alexandria, VA: TESOL, 1996.

Weaver, C. *Teaching Grammar in Context*. Portsmouth, NH: Boynton/Cook, 1996.

Wiggins, G. "Creating Tests Worth Taking," *Educational Leadership 49* (8) (1992): 26–33

Index